KENNETH C. DAVIS

ILLUSTRATED BY ROB SHEPPERSON

DON'T
KNOW
MUCH
ABOUT

Abraham
Lincoln

HarperCollins Publishers

Photo and Map Credits:

Page 83, Chicago Historical Society, ICHi-30998, 3/9/1861.
All other photographs courtesy of the Library of Congress.

Maps on pages 87 and 98 by Patricia Tobin.

This is a Don't Know Much About® book.

Don't Know Much About® is the registered trademark of Kenneth C. Davis.

Don't Know Much About® Abraham Lincoln

Copyright © 2004 by Kenneth C. Davis

Library of Congress Cataloging-in-Publication Data
Davis, Kenneth C.
Don't know much about Abraham Lincoln / Kenneth C. Davis ; illustrated by Rob
Shepperson.—1st ed.
p.   cm.
Summary: Examines the childhood and youth, education, law career, family life, and
presidency of Abraham Lincoln. Includes bibliographical references and index.
ISBN 0-06-028820-5 (lib. bdg.) — ISBN 0-06-442127-9 (pbk.)
1. Lincoln, Abraham, 1809–1865—Miscellanea—Juvenile literature. 2. Presidents—United
States—Miscellanea—Juvenile literature. [1. Lincoln, Abraham, 1809–1865. 2. Presidents.
3. Questions and answers.] I. Shepperson, Rob, ill. II. Title.
E457.905.D39 2004
973.7'092—dc21
2003009587

Design by Charles Yuen

1 2 3 4 5 6 7 8 9 10

First Edition

ACKNOWLEDGMENTS

An author's name goes on the cover of a book. But behind that book are a great many people who make it all happen. I would like to thank all the wonderful people at HarperCollins who helped make this book a reality, including Susan Katz, Kate Morgan Jackson, Barbara Lalicki, Martha Rago, Rosemary Brosnan, Amy Burton, Meredith Charpentier, Dana Hayward, Maggie Herold, Jeanne Hogle, Rachel Orr, and Lorelei Russ. I would also like to thank David Black, Joy Tutela, and Alix Reid for their friendship, assistance, and great ideas. My wife, Joann, and my children, Jenny and Colin, are always a source of inspiration, joy, and support, and without them my work would not be possible.

I especially thank Rodney O. Davis, codirector of the Lincoln Studies Center at Knox College, for reviewing the manuscript and providing helpful insights; Rob Shepperson for his striking illustrations; and Barry Varela for his unique contribution.

CONTENTS

This portrait of Lincoln appears on the
five-dollar bill.

Imagine rolling out of bed—a thin mattress filled with cornhusks—and putting your bare feet down on a cold dirt floor. A hot shower to start the day? Forget it. There isn't even a bathroom inside. There is no light in your one-room house, except for the first bits of rising sun coming through the cracks in the walls. And there is no fire in the fireplace yet, because it's your job to start it.

Once the fire is lit, you have other work to do. There are chickens to feed, water to fetch, wood to chop. And what about school? Maybe, if there is time and you don't have too many chores this morning.

It is hard to imagine life for Abraham Lincoln when he was growing up nearly two hundred years ago. It is also hard to imagine that a poor boy, with so little education, could grow up to become president.

Abraham Lincoln was elected during the greatest crisis in our country's history, when the arguments over slavery tore the nation in two, dividing families and friends. Born in a time when slavery was legal, Abraham Lincoln had always hated the idea that one person could own another. As time went by, Lincoln knew that America could not last as a nation if slavery was allowed to continue.

He served as president throughout the four terrible years of the Civil War, a war in which more than 600,000 soldiers—some of them boys between the ages of twelve and sixteen—were killed. Though Lincoln didn't know much about the army or being a soldier, he suffered as he watched these young men die in battle. The war left deep scars on America for a long time to come.

There are many stories about Abraham Lincoln that are myths or legends—many of them made up after he was killed, just days after the Civil War had ended. Some of these stories show that Lincoln was brave, honest, funny, and a great leader. All of those things are true, even if some of the legends are not. But this book tells the remarkable, *real* story about Lincoln—a poor boy who came from such simple beginnings and grew up to become the greatest of all presidents.

CHAPTER 1

"An Extra Good Boy"

A typical Kentucky log cabin

Was Abraham Lincoln really born in a log cabin?

When Abraham was born at home, on February 12, 1809, home was a one-room log cabin only eighteen feet long. His father, Thomas Lincoln, had built the cabin from trees he had cleared from his land—three hundred acres on the south fork of Nolin Creek, near Hodgenville, Kentucky. The gaps between the logs were filled with mud and straw. The floor was pounded dirt. There was one door with a leather hinge and one window with no glass, as well as a stone fireplace. The chimney was made of sticks coated with clay, to keep it from catching fire.

What were Abraham's parents like?

Lincoln's ancestors had come to Kentucky from Virginia, following the famous pioneer Daniel Boone, a distant relative. When Thomas Lincoln was only six, he saw an Indian kill his father, who'd been clearing a field. Thomas's older brother then shot and killed the Indian; otherwise Thomas might have been killed or kidnapped.

By his early teens, Thomas was on his own, earning his way in the world rather than going to school. Though he never learned to read very well and could barely write his own name, Thomas earned a living as a carpenter, framing houses and making furniture and coffins. Between carpentry jobs he took any work he could find—laboring on farms, fighting Indians, guarding prisoners at the small stone jailhouse where his friend was the jailer.

Thomas Lincoln was known as a fun-loving man who was the best storyteller around. In 1806 he married Nancy Hanks. Known for her kindness, cheerfulness, and hard work, she was also a deeply religious woman who valued education.

By the time their first child, Sarah, was born in 1807, Thomas Lincoln had saved enough money to buy his own property. The family eventually moved to Sinking Spring Farm, where Abraham Lincoln was born.

> **ABRAHAM, PLAIN AND SIMPLE**
>
> Abraham Lincoln was his full legal name—he had no middle name. He disliked the nickname "Abe."

How many states were united when Abraham was born?

In 1809, when Lincoln was born, Thomas Jefferson was president and there were only seventeen states in the Union. Ohio had been the latest state admitted, back in 1803. Kentucky, where the Lincolns were living, had been a state since 1792.

But in 1803 President Jefferson had made the Louisiana Purchase, buying a huge swath of the middle of the continent from France. So, although there were no states west of the Mississippi at the time of Lincoln's birth, the nation was growing.

What was life like for young Abraham Lincoln?

When Abraham was two years old, his family moved a few miles to another farm called Knob Creek Farm. It was one of many moves they would make. A year later Nancy Lincoln gave birth to another boy, named Thomas for his father. But he died within a few days. In those times many babies died in childbirth or soon after they were born, because the conditions were so hard. There were few doctors around, very little medicine was available, and people did not understand the importance of keeping clean.

Childhood on an American farm had not changed much since the days of the Pilgrims. There was work to be done, even by the youngest children. Boys took care of the animals and fields. Girls helped their mothers cook, clean, sew, and keep house. Almost everything that was used was made from scratch. There weren't many "store-bought" goods.

There were few neighbors and simple pastimes, such as fishing and swimming in summer. Of course, there was no television or radio or computers. Not even toys from stores.

You were expected to mind your manners and respect your elders. You'd get a whack with a switch when you didn't behave.

ᏖᏖ My earliest recollection is of the Knob Creek place. I remember that old home very well. Our farm was composed of three fields surrounded by high hills and deep gorges. Sometimes when there came a big rain, the water would come down through the gorges and spread all over the farm. The last thing I remember of doing there was one Saturday afternoon; the other boys planted the corn in what we called the big field; it contained seven acres—and I dropped the pumpkin seeds. I dropped two seeds every other hill and every other row. The next Sunday morning there came a big rain in the hills; it did not rain a drop in the valley, but the water coming through the gorges washed ground, corn, pumpkin seeds and all clear off the field. **ᏕᏕ**

—**Abraham Lincoln**, recalling his childhood

What is a "blab" school?

There were no public schools on the frontier in Lincoln's day. Children on isolated farms were taught to read at home by their parents. If there were enough families in a settlement, the parents might chip in to hire a teacher, who would hold classes in a simple one-room schoolhouse. Children of all ages would sit together and learn to read and "cipher," or do arithmetic. They all spoke out loud, or "blabbed," at the same time. That's why it was called a blab school. The idea was that if the students were talking, they wouldn't be daydreaming!

Although Thomas and Nancy Lincoln had little education, they knew the value of being able to read and write. They sent their children to school when they could. But teachers weren't always available, and money and time were tight.

Nevertheless, off and on, for a few days here, a few weeks there, Abraham and Sarah went to school at a log schoolhouse about two miles from home. Abraham learned the basic skills—how to read, write, and do a little arithmetic. By the time he was seven, he could read the Bible.

SCHOOLWORK SHOVEL?

A popular myth says that young Abraham practiced writing on the back of a shovel by the light of the fire.

Did it really happen? Probably not. While it's true that paper, quills, and ink were luxury items that wouldn't have been wasted on schoolchildren, young Abraham probably would have had something other than a shovel to write on. He might have used a chalk pencil on a slate board that could be wiped clean, as children had been doing for generations.

AMERICAN VOICES

66 Sometimes he would write with piece of charcoal, or the p'int of a burnt stick, on the fence or floor. We got a little paper at the country town, and I made ink out of blackberry juice. . . . I made his first pen out of a turkey buzzard feather. We hadn't no geese them days—to make good pens of goose quills. 99

—**Dennis Hanks**, a first cousin of Nancy Hanks Lincoln

How do we know about Lincoln's childhood?

Growing up, Lincoln wasn't famous. No one was taking notes on his day-to-day experiences. Later on Lincoln wrote a few short, autobiographical sketches, but he never gave a detailed account of his childhood.

Myths and stories about Lincoln—especially those centered on his youth—often come from books that were written shortly after he died. Some of the authors of these books interviewed old people who had known Lincoln years before. Of course, people's memories are not always trustworthy, and there's a natural inclination to exaggerate about famous people. Still, there was probably a good deal of truth in many of the stories told by those who knew him as a child.

❝Yes I remember Abe Lincoln well as a little bit of a fellow. . . . Abe and I went to the same school. My father, Zachariah Riney, was the teacher. . . .

"He was then barely seven years old and I was ten. I remember his big sister bringing him to school the first day. Oh, she was fond of him, she also attended school there; and all day long, whether at lessons or at play, her careful eye was constantly watching him. She was a regular little mother to him. . . .

"He wore home spun clothes as did all the children, and went barefooted. He never received a whipping and in our time the child was not spoiled by sparing the rod, and to go without a whipping a whole session was proof that he was an extra good boy. ❞
—**Susan Riney Yeager**, as an old woman in 1897, recalling Lincoln's school days

Why did the Lincolns leave Kentucky?

In those days, who owned what piece of frontier land was not always clear. A man would clear a field, build a cabin, and declare ownership of the wilderness all around, then sell it to someone else. Often there were competing claims of ownership.

When Abraham was seven, his father lost part of the land he thought he owned in a property dispute. Frustrated by legal battles over the land, Thomas

Lincoln moved the family west, to southern Indiana, where Abraham grew up to manhood.

Did Abraham see slaves when he was growing up?

Kentucky was a "slave state," meaning that it was legal for white people to own black people as slaves. Yet the small farms of central Kentucky, where the Lincolns lived, weren't like the great plantations of the Deep South, where tens or hundreds of slaves might be kept by a single family. Poor Kentucky farmers couldn't afford human property, and many opposed slavery on religious grounds.

It's likely that Abraham saw black slaves working the rivers and roads in Kentucky. In later life he claimed that opposition to slavery was one of the reasons his father moved the family to Indiana, a "free state" where slavery was illegal.

❝ [Thomas Lincoln] removed to what is now Spencer County, Indiana, in the autumn of 1816, Abraham then being in his eighth year. This removal was partly on account of slavery, but chiefly on account of the difficulty of land titles in Kentucky. . . . At this place Abraham took an early start as a hunter, which was never much improved afterward. A few days before the completion of his eighth year, in the absence of his father, a flock of wild turkeys approached the new log cabin, and Abraham with a rifle-gun, standing inside, shot through a crack and killed one of them. He has never since pulled a trigger on any larger game. ❞

—**Abraham Lincoln**, from a short autobiographical sketch cast in the third person. Lincoln wrote the sketch in 1860 at the request of a Chicago newspaperman who wanted to write a biography of the newly elected president.

What sad event occurred in 1818, when Abraham was nine years old?

His mother died suddenly of what the pioneers called "milk-sick," a common illness of the time. Young Abraham had to help build his mother's coffin, pull it through the snow on a sled to a hillside, and help bury her.

Naturally, he was heartbroken. "All that I am or ever hope to be, I owe to my angel mother," he said later in life.

When Nancy Lincoln died, Abraham's sister took over all of the household chores. Sarah tried hard, but she was only eleven. She was unable to do the job her mother had done. The house became messy and dirty. The family's clothes looked ragged. Something had to be done.

❝ She knew she was going to die and called the
children to her dying side and told them to be good
and kind to their father, to one another, and to the
world, expressing a hope that they might live as they
had been taught by her to love men, love reverence,
and worship God. Here in this rude house, of the
milk sickness, died one of the very best women in
the whole race, known for kindness, tenderness,
charity and love to the world. Mrs. Lincoln always
taught Abe goodness, kindness, read the good Bible to
him, taught him to read and to spell, taught him
sweetness and benevolence as well. . . . **❞**

—Dennis Hanks

POISONED MILK

The pioneers didn't know what caused milk-sick, though they knew
the illness was somehow connected to the drinking of cows' milk.
Nowadays we know that when cows eat certain plants, such as
rayless goldenrod or white snakeroot, poisons can pass into the
cows' milk. This makes the milk dangerous, even deadly, for people
to drink. Modern dairy farming techniques have eliminated this
problem, along with other diseases and impurities in milk.

Who saved the Lincolns from a life of squalor?

A little over a year after Nancy died, Thomas Lincoln
married a thirty-year-old widow named Sarah Bush
Johnston. Sarah had three children of her own:
Elizabeth, aged twelve; Matilda, aged ten; and John,
aged eight. Including a twenty-year-old cousin,
Dennis Hanks, whom the Lincolns had taken in,
their little cabin now was home to eight people.

Gradually, the Lincoln clan's fortunes improved.
Sarah Johnston Lincoln was a hard worker who

cooked and cleaned and kept everyone looking civilized. She made sure Abraham and the other children were able to attend blab school for a few weeks each year. Abraham quickly grew to love his kind and understanding stepmother. In later life he considered her to be as much his mother as his birth mother, Nancy, had been.

Abraham also grew to love his stepsisters and stepbrother. Though he would always mourn his birth mother, Abraham found happiness in the new, enlarged family of Lincolns and Johnstons.

What kinds of books did Abraham read?

By his own account, his formal schooling "did not amount to one year" in total. He read what few books he could get his hands on—first and foremost, the Bible. Other books probably included Daniel Defoe's *Robinson Crusoe*; John Bunyan's story of Christian faith, *Pilgrim's Progress*; and *Aesop's*

Fables. He was also fascinated by *The Arabian Nights.* By the fire Lincoln would read these tales of romance and adventure to Dennis and Sarah. Once Dennis said they were a "pack of lies." Lincoln answered, "Mighty fine lies."

Abraham had a special interest in history and the lives of great men. He probably read the famous biography of George Washington by Parson Weems that told the story (now known to be untrue) of the cherry tree. He would also have studied the important documents of the Revolutionary period, such as the Declaration of Independence and the Constitution.

A small list, perhaps— but what Abraham read he absorbed thoroughly, especially the rich cadences of the Bible. He was acutely aware of the limits of his education. In later life he turned this awareness to good use by poking fun at himself for his ignorance, winning people over with his humility and good humor.

CHAPTER 2

The Rail-splitter

Lincoln, the Rail Splitter, by J. L. G. Ferris

What did Abraham do during his teenage years?

Work, work, and more work. Mostly physical labor. In later life one of his nicknames was "The Rail-splitter," because he'd spent so much time chopping wood into rails for fences. The image of the young Lincoln wielding an ax lives on today.

But it wasn't mere image. Lincoln really did spend countless hours laboring on his father's farm—chopping down trees, pulling stumps, clearing the land.

❝Upon leaving Kentucky in 1816, when Abraham was seven, Thomas Lincoln settled in an unbroken forest, and the clearing away of surplus wood was the great task ahead. Abraham, though very young, was large of his age, and had an ax put into his hands at once; and from that till within his twenty-third year he was almost constantly handling that most useful instrument—less, of course, in plowing and harvesting seasons.❞

—**Lincoln**, from his 1860 autobiographical sketch

As he grew to be a young man, what did he look like?

Tall—extraordinarily so. By the time he was sixteen, he stood six feet tall. He'd be six feet four inches tall when full grown. This was in an age when the average man was little more than five and a half feet tall!

Long arms, long legs. A shock of unruly black hair. Dark eyes and a sad face. He often joked about his homeliness. But his appearance was memorable, to say the least. He literally stood head and shoulders above the crowd.

LANKY LINCOLN

Lincoln was famous for poking fun at his homely features. These quips are attributed to him:

"Common-looking people are the best in the world. That is the reason the Lord makes so many of them."

"I have stepped out upon this platform that I may see you and that you may see me, and in the arrangement I have the best of the bargain."

"If I were two-faced, would I be wearing this one?"

Abraham was strong too. Years of steering the plow, lifting bushels and bales, and swinging a heavy ax had hardened his body. He was wiry, with surprisingly powerful arms and large hands that could grip hard. One Lincoln legend says he once picked up a six-hundred-pound chicken coop and moved it.

How did Abraham first see something outside the little world of rural Indiana?

When he was seventeen, Abraham got a job at the ferry landing where Anderson Creek joins the Ohio River near Troy, Indiana. As he loaded and unloaded the ferryboat for thirty-seven cents a day, Abraham watched the barges, rafts, and flatboats, as well as steamboats belching their plumes of black smoke. He felt the urge to join the traders, trappers, and other travelers who sailed up and down the river.

In 1828, when Abraham was nineteen, he and a friend, Allen Gentry, built a crude flatboat. Allen's father hired them to take a load of farm produce to New Orleans, selling and trading along the way.

We don't know exactly what they saw or did on this trip, though they must have had many adventures. Abraham later wrote that one night they were attacked by a gang. He and Allen drove the wrong-doers off the boat and escaped by floating away.

In New Orleans they sold the rest of the cargo and the flatboat itself, then returned to Indiana by steamboat. Abraham had earned twenty-four dollars, which he turned over to his father.

The trip down the river opened Lincoln's eyes to the wider world—a world with big cities, bustling marketplaces, fancy houses, and educated men. He also would have seen some of the terrible injustice of slavery. New Orleans was the site of one of the South's largest slave markets, where black men, women, and children were auctioned off to the highest bidder.

It must have been hard for Lincoln to return to his father's sleepy farm. But return he did, staying on for another two years.

United States slave trade, 1830

❝ The slaves are put in stalls like the pens they use for cattle—a man and his wife with a child on each arm. And there's a curtain, sometimes just a sheet over the front of the stall, so the bidders can't see the 'stock' too soon. The overseer's standin' just outside with a big black snake whip and a pepperbox pistol in his belt. Across the square a little piece, there's a big platform with steps leadin' to it.

"When the slaves is on the platform—what they calls the 'block'—the overseer yells, 'Tom or Jason, show the bidders how you walk.' Then, the slave steps across the platform, and the biddin' starts. **❞**

—**James Martin**, in a 1937 interview, recalling a slave auction. Martin was born a slave in Virginia in 1847.

If Abraham was thriving, how was the rest of the family faring?

Not so well. In January 1828, not long before Abraham's trip to New Orleans, his beloved sister, Sarah, had died in childbirth. Then milk-sick hit the family again, but luckily no one died. In 1830 Thomas Lincoln sold the farm and loaded the household onto three wagons. Abraham drove one of the ox teams that took the family the two hundred miles to their new home: Illinois.

How did Abraham finally strike out on his own?

When the Lincolns moved, Abraham was twenty-one years old—now a full-grown man. It was time for him to make his own way in the world. Though he wasn't afraid of hard physical labor, a childhood spent on a frontier farm had convinced him that he didn't want to follow in his father's footsteps.

In 1831 Abraham decided to make another flatboat trip to New Orleans, this time with his stepbrother, John Johnston, and his cousin John Hanks. The three young men hired themselves out to a local businessman named Denton Offutt, who paid them to build the boat and take it downstream.

Early in the journey the boat became stuck going over a milldam in the Sangamon River. Water flowed over the back end of the boat, which began to sink. Lincoln suggested drilling a hole in the boat to let the water drain out. The idea worked, and the crew was able to shove the boat over the dam.

Offutt, who had been along for the first part of the journey, was impressed by Lincoln's quick thinking. When Lincoln returned from the trip, Offutt offered him a job at the very mill whose dam had almost capsized the flatboat. The mill, and the store attached to it, were located in the small settlement of New Salem, Illinois.

Lincoln earned fifteen dollars a month running Offutt's mill and store. It wasn't a grand salary, but he lived rent free in a small room at the back of the store. New Salem was to be his home for the next six years. He had left his father's house for good.

Who were the Clary's Grove Boys?

In the 1830s New Salem was a rough-and-tumble settlement of about twenty-five buildings, basically strung out along two sides of a dusty street. There was a tavern, a blacksmithy, a cooper (barrel-making) shop, a few general stores, a schoolhouse, a sawmill, a gristmill, and not much else.

Denton Offutt liked to brag that his young employee could outjump, outrun, and outwrestle anyone around. The boast soon reached the ears of a gang of young toughs called the Clary's Grove Boys. Offutt made a ten-dollar bet over the outcome of a wrestling match between Lincoln and the Clary's Grove Boys' leader, Jack Armstrong.

The whole town gathered to watch the fight. There was drinking and gambling. Lincoln and Armstrong grabbed at each other. For a minute they grappled, neither gaining the advantage.

According to some versions of the story, Lincoln lifted Armstrong off his feet, shook him, and tossed him to the ground. The rest of Armstrong's gang started at Lincoln, who said he'd whip them all—one at a time. No one took him up on it.

Other versions have the match ending in a draw. Still another has Armstrong winning, but only because he cheated. In any case Jack Armstrong, the toughest man around, had to admit he couldn't beat Abraham Lincoln in a fair fight.

The Clary's Grove Boys took Lincoln on as their new leader, and he and Armstrong became good friends. Lincoln became a calming influence on the former hooligans, and they supported him in return. Armstrong even let Lincoln live in his house when he was short on money.

Lincoln had shown he was strong—but was he smart, too?

Though Lincoln never looked down on men who worked with their hands, he wanted to work with his mind. To that end he tried to improve his math skills and studied the rules of grammar. He read Shakespeare and the poetry of Robert Burns.

Even in a town as small and remote as New Salem, there were men with intellectual aspirations in nineteenth-century America. Lincoln joined the New Salem Debating Society, where he met men who had attended college. Despite his lack of education, he soon impressed his fellow debaters with his quick wit, eloquent speechmaking, and logical mind.

AMERICAN VOICES

❝ As he arose to speak, his tall form towered above the little assembly. Both hands were thrust down deep in the pockets of his pantaloons. A perceptible smile at once lit up the faces of the audience, for all anticipated the relation of some humorous story. But he opened up the discussion in splendid style, to the infinite astonishment of his friends. As he warmed with his subject his hands would forsake his pockets and would enforce his ideas by awkward gestures;

but would very soon seek their easy resting place. He pursued the question with reason and argument so pithy and forcible that all were amazed. . . . The president [of the Debating Society], at his fireside after the meeting, remarked to his wife that there was more than wit and fun in Abe's head; that he was already a fine speaker; that all he lacked was culture. **99**

—**R. B. Rutledge** on Lincoln's first performance before the New Salem Debating Society, in an 1866 letter

What was Lincoln's first taste of politics?

You might think a young man, only twenty-three and just off the farm, would get his feet wet by working on another man's campaign. Or if he was going to run for office himself, he might aim low at first. But no, Lincoln thought big. With no prior experience, he announced in March 1832 that he would run for a spot in the Illinois state legislature!

Did he run as a Democrat or Republican?

Neither. In fact, the Republican Party didn't exist yet.

When Lincoln first entered politics, the Democrats and the Whigs were the two main political parties. But these political parties were very disorganized in the early 1830s, especially on the frontier. They had little influence on elections. Men ran for office simply by announcing themselves and declaring what they stood for. Sometimes a candidate would proclaim himself a follower of a famous national figure.

Lincoln let it be known that he was a follower of the Kentucky politician Henry Clay (1777–1852). Like Clay, he believed government should help businesses grow by building roads and canals and making other internal improvements. Lincoln was convinced that the nation's future lay in innovation, progress, and industry.

Lincoln's platform for state legislature stressed practical issues, including the importance of education and the local transportation system. But to voters, Lincoln's personal reputation—and who his friends were—mattered more than his political philosophy.

DEMOCRAT OR WHIG?

The Democrats followed President Andrew Jackson (1767–1845), the extremely popular hero of the War of 1812 who had also been born in a log cabin. Jackson's Democrats held to the ideas of Thomas Jefferson, who disliked big government and favored a society of small, independent farmers and craftsmen.

The Whigs carried on the tradition of former Treasurer Alexander Hamilton and former President John Quincy Adams, both of whom had favored a strong, active government that could promote industry and transportation. Whigs also simply feared and disliked Jackson personally—they felt that he had claimed too much power for the presidency. The leaders of the Whigs were Henry Clay and Daniel Webster (1782–1852).

Though he had yet to declare himself a member of any party, Lincoln, as a follower of Henry Clay, was on his way to becoming a Whig.

Why did Lincoln join the army?

Since the first Europeans came to settle America, Indians had lost ground. In 1805 the U.S. government forced the Sauk and Fox Indians to move from their ancestral lands in northern Illinois. They were sent west, across the Mississippi River, to what later became Iowa Territory.

In 1832 about a thousand Sauk and Fox men, women, and children, led by Black Hawk, moved back into northern Illinois. White settlers panicked. Skirmishes broke out, and within months all-out war was declared by the U.S. government on Black Hawk's followers.

When the governor of Illinois asked for volunteers to fight the Black Hawk War, Lincoln enlisted. Offutt's mill and store were about to go out of business, and Lincoln (despite the fact that he was running for the state legislature) had no immediate prospects. A stint in the Illinois militia seemed like a good idea.

Lincoln was elected captain by the men of his company—the first time he won an election of any kind. Later he said that, since winning that honor, he had not had "any success in life which gave him so much satisfaction."

He spent about two and a half months in the regiment, seeing no action but gaining from the experience nonetheless. He made some new friends and learned how to lead men. Lincoln once joked of a political rival who claimed to be a war hero, "If he saw any live, fighting Indians, it was more than I did; but I had a good many bloody struggles with the musquitoes [sic]."

The army chased Black Hawk into Wisconsin, where nearly all his followers were massacred in August 1832. Black Hawk escaped, but was captured not long after. He was eventually forced to return to Iowa, where he lived until 1838.

AMERICAN VOICES

❝ Why did the Great Spirit ever send the whites to this island to drive us from our homes and introduce among us poisonous liquors, disease and death? They should have remained in the land the Great Spirit allotted them. ❞

—from *The Autobiography of Ma-Ka-Tai-Me-She-Kia-Kiak, or Black Hawk,* published in 1833

Was Lincoln elected to the legislature?

Lincoln had very little time to campaign for state legislature when he returned home from war. In the August election he came in eighth out of thirteen candidates. But in the New Salem district, he received 277 out of 300 votes. Lincoln was encouraged by the result: people who knew him liked him. His problem was that, outside the immediate New Salem area, no one knew him.

Lincoln wasn't easily discouraged. Many years later, after another electoral setback, he supposedly said,

"I feel somewhat like the boy in Kentucky who stubbed his toe while running to see his sweetheart. The boy said he was too big to cry, and far too badly hurt to laugh."

Despite the defeat, Lincoln knew he would run again.

Out of the army, with no job . . . what was next for Lincoln?

Lincoln decided he'd like to go into business for himself. With a man named William F. Berry, Lincoln bought a general store in New Salem on credit. There he sold goods such as tea, coffee, sugar, salt, crockery, and calico.

Lincoln took odd jobs—splitting rails, laboring on farms, surveying, and so on—to earn extra cash. He also served as postmaster for the town, a position that brought him a little extra money, about fifty-five dollars a year. Handling the mail gave him a chance to read lots of newspapers. His knowledge of local and national events grew.

PRESIDENTIAL SURVEY

Three great presidents—George Washington, Thomas Jefferson, and Abraham Lincoln—were employed as surveyors in their youth. A surveyor would measure plots of land, mark boundaries of property, and draw maps. In a large country with few reliable signs and maps, this was a very important job.

Was Lincoln a good shopkeeper?

The store was a disaster. Lincoln wasn't one to drive a hard bargain, and his partner, Berry, had a drinking problem. The store lost money steadily and went out of business in little over a year. When Berry died, Lincoln was left with over a thousand dollars' debt—quite a lot of money in those days. It took him years to pay off what he owed, but in the end he did. That kind of fair dealing earned him the nickname "Honest Abe."

His reputation also helped his next try for office. In 1834 he declared himself a Whig and won the election as a state representative. Lincoln's political career had really begun.

> **MILES FOR MONEY**
>
> You might have heard the story of how Lincoln, as a young shopkeeper in New Salem, walked three miles to return a few cents to a customer he'd accidentally shortchanged.
>
> Did it really happen? No one knows for sure, but this story might actually be true. People who knew Lincoln all agreed that he was unusually honest. It's not unlikely that he would have gone out of his way to return money he knew didn't belong to him.

Was Lincoln's first term in the legislature a success?

Borrowing two hundred dollars for expenses (including a sixty-dollar suit), Lincoln set out for Vandalia, the state capital, in November 1834.

Being state representative was not a full-time job. The legislature met for only a few short weeks every other winter. Unlike many modern-day politicians, state legislators in Lincoln's day had to keep their regular jobs back home.

During the term, representatives would debate, form alliances, write bills, and pass them into law or defeat them. Lincoln was actively involved, giving speeches and even introducing some minor bills.

He returned home with a payment of $258 in his pocket—enough to repay the loan for his expenses and to have a little left over.

Lincoln was a popular representative; he was reelected three times: in 1836, 1838, and 1840.

❝ [Lincoln had] raw-boned, angular features deeply furrowed, ungraceful—almost uncouth, having little, if any of that polish so important in society life. Yet there was a magnetism and dash about the man that made him a universal favorite. Underneath that rough exterior, it was easy to find out—dwelt a mind and a heart of immense powers. ❞
—**Vandalia resident**, recalling the new state legislator years later

VANDALIA
AND THE LONG NINE

Vandalia was the first state capital of Illinois. Lincoln and eight other legislators succeeded in having the state capital moved north to Springfield in 1839, where it still is today. All of these legislators happened to be tall, so the group was known as the Long Nine.

What did Lincoln do back in New Salem?

Lincoln spent most of his time working hard—earning money to support himself and reading to improve himself. By nature Lincoln was a sociable fellow, though he had a dark, melancholic streak. (He was prone to depression.) Unlike many young men on the frontier, Lincoln wasn't much of a drinker. By the time he'd moved to New Salem, he wouldn't touch alcohol.

His bout with Jack Armstrong had proven him to be a good fighter, and Lincoln continued to enjoy physical competition of all kinds: footraces, wrestling matches, weight-lifting contests. He liked to talk, swap stories, and dance. He attended meetings of the Debating Society as well as such frontier social events as barn raisings and square dances.

Who was Ann Rutledge?

Legend has it that Lincoln fell in love with a young woman from New Salem named Ann Rutledge. She returned his love in full even though she was engaged to another. When Ann died suddenly in 1835, probably of typhoid fever, Lincoln's heart was broken. He was so saddened that he thought about suicide and nearly went insane. He was never the same again. Or so the story goes.

In truth, there's no documentary evidence to support the story. Lincoln never mentioned Ann Rutledge in his letters or other writings. It was only after Lincoln was elected president that people came forward claiming to remember the tragic New Salem romance from thirty years before.

So did Lincoln lose the love of his life? Maybe, maybe not. It's a romantic story that lots of people like to believe. But there's no way of knowing now whether it was true or not.

CHAPTER 3

A Mighty Fine Lawyer

Lincoln the Lawyer by Frederick T. Stuart

What law school did Lincoln attend?

While supporting himself with his postmastering and the usual assortment of odd jobs, Lincoln decided to become a lawyer. In those days you didn't have to go to law school. You just had to show some familiarity with the law by passing a simple bar exam. If the other members of the local bar association liked you, they declared you a lawyer and you could set up shop.

Lincoln had been studying borrowed law books off and on for several years. After his first session in the legislature, he threw himself wholeheartedly into the study of law. In his spare time and during breaks from work, he read Blackstone's *Commentaries*. This book explains the law in England, which forms the basis of much of the American system.

WHAT DOES IT MEAN?

Does a bar exam test a person's knowledge of mixed drinks? No. Here, the *bar* refers to the practice of law. A bar exam tests a person's knowledge of the law.

In September 1836 Lincoln passed the bar exam and received his license to practice law. The local lawyers and judges were happy to welcome him to the profession.

FLYING PAPERS

As postmaster Lincoln got into the habit of carrying letters in the band around his hat. Later, after he'd become a lawyer, he stored legal papers inside the sweatband of his hat.

One story goes that some boys decided to play a prank on him. They tied a string across a street high enough for most people to walk under with no problem.

When the very tall Lincoln came along, wearing his tall stovepipe hat, the string caught the hat. The papers and hat went flying, and the boys jumped out laughing from where they were hiding. Always a good sport, Lincoln laughed along with them.

Did it really happen? Possibly, but not probably. Lincoln really did store papers in his hat. But the story of the boys' hat trick is likely just a "tall" tale.

❝ If you wish to be a lawyer, attach no consequence to the *place* you are in, or the *person* you are with; but get books, sit down anywhere, and go to reading for yourself. That will make a lawyer of you quicker than any other way. **❞**

—**Lincoln**, from an 1858 letter to a young man who had applied for a job at Lincoln's firm

Why did Lincoln move to Springfield?

By the late 1830s, it was obvious that the Sangamon River was too shallow for regular boat traffic. (Remember, Lincoln had first come to New Salem because the flatboat he was working on had got stuck on the milldam.) New Salem depended on the river for trade. As river traffic died, stores and businesses failed.

Lincoln saw that if he was going to have a successful law practice, he'd have to go where the action was. And that was the new state capital, Springfield.

By 1840 New Salem had turned into a ghost town.

How did Lincoln meet his wife?

Mary Ann Todd was born in Kentucky in 1818. The Todds were a large, well-off, and socially prominent family accustomed to owning slaves. Growing up, Mary lived in comfort, learned French, and studied such "female arts" as music and dancing.

In the fall of 1839, Mary moved to her sister Elizabeth's house in Springfield, Illinois. Elizabeth was married to Ninian Edwards. Ninian was Abraham's friend, an important Whig member of the legislature and one of the Long Nine.

Soon after she moved, Mary met Abraham at a dance. Supposedly his first words to her were "Miss Todd, I want to dance with you in the worst way." She reportedly told friends later, "Mr. Lincoln danced just the way he said he would . . . in the worst way."

Coming from a well-to-do family, Mary Todd had a polish that Lincoln lacked. She was quick-witted and lively; some said she could be sarcastic and cutting, too. Lincoln was immediately drawn to her intelligence and spirit.

At only five feet two, with a squarish, blocky face and figure, Mary Todd made quite a contrast to the lean, lanky Lincoln. Nevertheless, they entered into an on-again, off-again, three-year courtship.

Why did Lincoln nearly fight a duel?

In the summer of 1842 several letters signed "Rebecca" appeared in a Springfield newspaper. They made fun of an important local politician, James Shields. Abraham submitted the first letter, but Mary Todd and her friend Julia Jayne had written two others without him knowing.

When Shields demanded that the newspaper editor reveal who wrote the letters, Lincoln came forward, without mentioning Mary and her friend. The hotheaded Shields promptly challenged Lincoln to a duel.

Surprised, Lincoln accepted the challenge and chose "cavalry broadswords of the largest size" as the weapon. Luckily the duel never came off. Mutual friends intervened at the last minute to patch up the disagreement before anyone was injured.

The incident did have one good effect. In the months preceding the event, Abraham and Mary Todd

"THE HYPO"

In 1841, shortly after Lincoln and Mary Todd had broken off their engagement, some of his friends thought Lincoln was "crazy as a loon." Some even considered him suicidal. At times Lincoln would not get out of bed. He did not eat. He lost weight. "Hypochondria" was the going term for unstable and emotionally disturbed behavior, what we might call "clinical depression" today.

The "hypo," as Lincoln called it, had him in its grip. A doctor finally suggested a change of scenery to ease Lincoln's dark state of mind, and during a visit with friends in Louisville he came out of his depression. However, he did continue to suffer milder bouts of the "hypo" throughout his life.

had called off their courtship. But writing the sarcastic letters to the editor, keeping a secret, cooking up the silly conditions for the duel—all this merriment had served to bring them back together. A few months later, on November 4, 1842, they were married at the home of Ninian and Elizabeth Edwards.

AMERICAN VOICES

❝ Nothing new here, except my marrying, which to me, is a matter of profound wonder. **❞**
—**Lincoln**, in a letter written a week after his wedding

What did a lawyer do on the frontier?

Lincoln continued working as a circuit lawyer to support himself and his new wife. For two and a half months at a stretch, each spring and fall, he'd ride from one county courthouse to the next, completing a circuit of fifteen courthouses. Since each courthouse was open for only a few days, the lawyers and judges worked frantically, trying to resolve six months' worth of cases before moving on to the next county.

Most of the cases involved everyday matters— property disputes, bad debts, fistfights, public drunkenness. Occasionally there were more lively cases—murders, robberies, scandalous divorces. The atmosphere was almost festive as people came from miles around to get the news at the courthouse.

While on the circuit, Lincoln lived with other traveling lawyers in cheap boardinghouses or taverns, two to a bed and half a dozen to a room.

Traveling, working, and living with his fellow lawyers, Lincoln became well known to a large number of influential Illinoisans. In 1844 he added a new partner, William H. Herndon, to his practice.

AMERICAN VOICES

❝ When he reached the office, about nine o'clock in the morning, the first thing he did was to pick up a newspaper, spread himself out on an old sofa, one leg on a chair, and read aloud, much to my discomfort. Singularly enough Lincoln never read any other way but aloud. ❞

—**William H. Herndon**, from *Life of Lincoln*, by William H. Herndon and Jesse W. Weik, 1889. Lincoln never outgrew the habit, first instilled in blab school, of reading aloud to himself.

❝ You have a good case, technically, but in terms of justice and equity, it's got problems. So you'll have to look for another lawyer to handle the case, because the whole time I was up there talking to the jury, I'd be thinking, 'Lincoln, you're a liar!' and I might just forget myself and say it out loud. ❞

—attributed to **Lincoln**, in turning down a potential client

Who was Stephen Douglas?

Born in Vermont in 1813, Stephen Douglas was to become one of the nation's most important politicians in the years before the Civil War.

Lincoln first met Douglas in a general store in Springfield, where men met to talk about political issues. Called "the Little Giant" because he was only five feet four inches tall, Douglas won election to the state legislature just a year after moving to Illinois. In that brief time, he had established a thriving law practice and made a name for himself by delivering a rousing speech before a large meeting of Democrats.

What caused the Mexican War?

For hundreds of years, Texas had been considered part of Mexico. In the 1820s, under the leadership of Stephen Austin, several hundred families from the United States moved to Texas and established a colony. In less than ten years, "American" Texans greatly outnumbered "Mexican" Texans. American Texans spoke English, were Protestant by religion, and owned slaves; Mexican Texans spoke Spanish, were Catholic, and opposed slavery. The two groups couldn't get along.

In 1836 the American Texans, led by Sam Houston, fought a successful war of independence from Mexico. For about a decade Texas was an independent country, though Mexico never recognized it as such.

In late 1845 Texas applied to become the twenty-eighth state of the Union. Mexico wasn't happy with

American forces, under General Winfield Scott, landing in Vera Cruz

this turn of events, especially since it was clear that the U.S. president, the Democrat James K. Polk, wanted to take over two more Mexican territories, New Mexico and California. In 1846 war broke out between Mexico and the United States.

What was Lincoln's next step?

In 1846 Lincoln ran for a seat in the U.S. House of Representatives. During the race for the nomination, Lincoln may have privately expressed the feeling that U.S. policy toward Mexico was unwise as well as unfair. But he was careful about what he said in public. The war was popular, and to have spoken out against it might have seemed unpatriotic.

In the end Lincoln won the nomination and easily won the August election.

Did Lincoln ever speak out against the war?

By December 1847, when Lincoln went to Washington, the fighting was over, and Mexico had lost. It was forced to recognize Texas as part of the United States. Mexico lost over five hundred thousand square miles of territory, including all of the future states of California, Nevada, and Utah, almost all of New Mexico and Arizona, and parts of Colorado and Wyoming.

Now safely in office, Lincoln made his opposition to the war public despite its popularity in Illinois. "It is a fact," he said, "that the United States Army, in marching to the Rio Grande, marched into a peaceful Mexican settlement, and frightened the inhabitants away from their homes and their growing crops." He believed President Polk had started the war as a ploy to win votes.

Democratic newspapers in Illinois called Lincoln a traitor and promised he'd never be elected again.

What was Manifest Destiny?

Literally, *manifest* means "self-evident" or "obvious." *Destiny* refers to what is fated to happen. So *manifest destiny* means the obvious thing that must happen.

To many Americans at this time, the manifest destiny of the United States was to expand west until the whole continent, from the Atlantic to the Pacific Ocean, was part of the nation. According to these *expansionists*, the creation of a continental United States was inevitable—God wanted it that way.

The Mexican War was **"**One of the most unjust ever waged by a stronger against a weaker nation. **"**

—Lieutenant **Ulysses S. Grant** on the Mexican War

What issues were facing the U.S. Congress during Lincoln's term?

Sometimes winning causes problems. The new land acquired in the Mexican War forced Congress to think about the problem of slavery all over again.

In the late 1840s, a minority of northerners thought slavery was immoral. These *abolitionists* called for the immediate end to it. Others, who had no moral objection to slavery, believed enslaved labor hurt free white workers. If a rich man could own a black man and force him to work for free, there was no need to pay the wages of a white man. So for different reasons, most northerners who had strong opinions wanted to keep slaves and slavery out of the western territories.

> ## COMPROMISING POSITION
>
> The issue of slavery had threatened to split the nation along north-south lines in 1819. Southern congressmen had wanted Missouri admitted as a slave state; northerners wanted it free. Basically the Missouri Compromise of 1820 admitted Missouri as a slave state but said that slavery would be banned in the remainder of the Louisiana Purchase north of latitude 36°30', the southern boundary of Missouri.

Many southerners felt that critics of slavery were attacking the culture of the South itself. Some of them declared slavery was a blessing: it had civilized "savage Africans" and guaranteed them a lifetime of food, housing, and employment. Seeing nothing wrong with slavery, many southerners wanted to keep it legal, at least in the southern territories.

About one-quarter of southerners owned slaves, but only a few masters of large plantations owned more than a hundred. Although most southern farmers couldn't afford to buy and keep slaves, they often thought slavery was acceptable. The Constitution allowed it. There were also many people who feared what would happen if the slaves were freed. There had been violent slave uprisings throughout the South. Many men said that their wives and daughters would not be safe if black men were free. That was a common argument that was used to inspire fear among all southern whites.

QUICK FACTS ABOUT SLAVERY

- The first Africans were brought to America in 1619 to the English colony of Jamestown, Virginia.

- Almost seven hundred thousand slaves were brought to English North America, and later the United States, during the two centuries of the slave trade; probably about that same number died in transit.

- In 1850 nine out of ten blacks lived in the South. Approximately one out of three southerners was black. In some states slaves outnumbered whites.

- By the outbreak of the Civil War, there were about four million slaves in the Confederacy.

Where did Lincoln stand on the issue of slavery?

Though Lincoln personally found the idea of slavery offensive, he admitted that the Constitution gave southerners a legal right to own slaves.

Like many other Americans, Lincoln believed slavery would eventually die a natural death: if left to their own devices, southerners would come to abolish slavery on their own. Washington and Jefferson had believed the same thing. So Lincoln preferred not to force abolition on the slaveholders. He feared that forcing the South to give up slavery would cause more problems than it would solve.

While acknowledging that slavery was untouchable where it existed, Lincoln believed it should not spread. He completely opposed allowing slavery in the territory won from Mexico or in any of the new states that would eventually be created. Time and time again, he voted to outlaw slavery in the western territory. But the question of slavery moving west was not settled, and the issue would become a key point in the presidential election of 1848.

Welcome to WESTERN TERRITORIES
SLAVERY TOLERATED
(by owners)

Who did Lincoln vote for in 1848?

Of the three main candidates only one opposed the extension of slavery into the territories. Surprisingly, he was not the man Lincoln campaigned for.

Lewis Cass, the Democratic nominee, sidestepped the issue by calling for "popular sovereignty," which meant that the territorial governments, not the U.S. Congress or the president, would decide for themselves whether to allow slavery or not.

The Whig nominee was Mexican War hero General Zachary Taylor of Louisiana. "Old Rough and Ready," as he was called, was the Whigs' best hope: his military record would appeal to northerners, while the fact that he owned slaves would reassure southerners. More soldier than politician, Taylor declined to give any opinion on the future of slavery in the territories.

Only the third-party candidate, former president Martin Van Buren of the Free-Soilers, took a clear position. Free-Soilers were against slavery—but they were not abolitionists. They wanted to see the western territories given away to free white men. In fact, some Free-Soilers wanted to bar all blacks, whether slave or free, from the western territories.

As a Whig, Lincoln campaigned vigorously for Taylor. With Cass and Van Buren splitting the Democratic vote, General Taylor took the election.

What did Lincoln do after campaigning for Taylor?

Lincoln returned to Washington to finish out his term in Congress, which ended in March 1849.

Debate in Congress still centered on what to do about slavery in the new territories. Texas had been admitted as a slave state. It appeared likely that New Mexico and California would be free states. Southerners, led by the firebrand John C. Calhoun, promised not to allow California in the Union at all if it insisted on being a free state. Some southern radicals threatened to *secede*, or leave the Union, if they lost California. Harsh words, even a fistfight, broke out on the floor of Congress.

After all the debate, the session closed with the fate of slavery in the territories still undecided. As Lincoln packed to return to Illinois, he was aware that there were no easy answers.

THE WIZARD OF SPRINGFIELD?

In 1849 Lincoln applied for, and won, a patent for a device to lift boats over sandbars and other obstacles. Apparently he'd been chewing on the problem ever since 1831, when he helped Denton Offutt's flatboat get over the New Salem milldam. According to the patent application, the invention used "adjustable buoyant air chambers" to raise a boat out of the water.

William H. Herndon later joked, "The invention was never applied to any vessel, so far as I ever learned, and the threatened revolution in steamboat architecture and navigation never came to pass."

Still, Lincoln is the only president ever to hold a patent.

CHAPTER 4

Birth of a Party

Mary, Robert, Tad, and Abraham Lincoln at home

Back in Springfield, what did Lincoln do?

Now almost forty years old, Lincoln was still interested in self-improvement. While working as a lawyer, he studied books on astronomy, taught himself geometry, read even more Shakespeare, and deepened his understanding of the Bible.

In 1843 Mary and Abraham had their first child, a son. Robert Lincoln inherited his mother's build. "Bob is short and low and, I expect, always will be," Abraham wrote of his three-year-old son. Quiet and shy, Robert had neither his mother's cutting wit nor his father's outgoing nature. Still, he was a thoughtful child who did well at school. In 1846 Mary gave birth to a second son, Edward, and in 1850 she had a third boy, William.

The early 1850s were a relatively peaceful period in Lincoln's life. His law practice brought in enough money to keep the family comfortable. He was well respected in the community. He had served his state and country honorably, and he looked forward to a long and productive life as a private citizen.

The years were not without sadness, however. Abraham and Mary's second child, Edward, died in 1850, probably of tuberculosis, at the age of three.

The next year Thomas Lincoln died. Abraham had never been close to his father and did not attend the funeral. Still, the death of his father must have been hard on him, as well as on his beloved stepmother, Sarah Johnston Lincoln. In the years that followed, Abraham always made sure that Sarah was comfortable and well cared for.

Meanwhile, in the world at large, things were happening that would have huge consequence for the fate of the nation generally and Abraham Lincoln personally.

AMERICAN VOICES

66 Angel Boy—fare thee well, farewell,
Sweet Eddie, we bid thee adieu!
Affection's wail cannot reach thee now
Deep though it be, and true. 99
— **Mary Todd Lincoln**, from her poem "To Little Eddie," written a week after the death of her son

What was the Compromise of 1850?

In the late 1840s, four unresolved problems, all having to do with slavery, plagued Congress:

• Would slavery be allowed into the territories won in the Mexican War?

• California had applied for admission to the Union as a free state. Should it be admitted?

• Texas, a slave state, claimed land as far west as Santa Fe (in what is now New Mexico). Was its claim legitimate?

• Washington, D.C., was home to the country's largest slave market. Should slavery remain legal in the nation's capital?

Henry Clay proposed a series of bills, known collectively as the Compromise of 1850, that would solve all four problems at once. He suggested that:

• The territories of Utah and New Mexico (which included the land that would later become Arizona and Nevada) would be allowed to decide the slavery question for themselves.

• California would be admitted to the Union as a free state.

• In exchange for $10 million from the federal government, Texas would give up its claim on land that became part of New Mexico.

• The Washington slave market would be shut down, but ownership of slaves would remain legal in the capital.

In addition, for allowing California to enter the Union as a free state, southerners would be granted passage of the extremely controversial Fugitive Slave Act.

Why was the Fugitive Slave Act so controversial?

Prior to the Compromise of 1850, if a slave escaped to freedom in the northern states, he could not be forced to return to bondage in the South. The Underground Railroad—a loosely organized network of individuals and groups—was able to usher thousands of runaway slaves to freedom in the North and Canada.

The Fugitive Slave Act stiffened the penalties against people caught helping runaway slaves. Worse, all it took to get any black person in the North deported to the South was the sworn testimony of one slave catcher and one "master." Blacks were not allowed to testify in their own defense. The commissioner was paid five dollars if he ruled for the accused slave; if he ruled for the master, he earned ten.

Abolitionists were outraged by the Fugitive Slave Act. Many white northerners who had never given much thought to the question of slavery now turned against the South.

What did Lincoln think of the Compromise of 1850?

He had seen how the dispute over slavery in the territories was threatening to tear Congress—and the country—apart. Despite the inclusion of the hateful Fugitive Slave Act, the compromise seemed to Lincoln to be the best hope to keep the country together.

How did a runaway slave become one of the most influential and famous men in America?

Frederick Douglass

Born into slavery on Maryland's Eastern Shore, Frederick Douglass (1817-1895) learned to read while living in Baltimore as a boy. At the age of twenty, he escaped to Massachusetts with his wife. He joined an abolitionist society and soon became known as a powerful and eloquent speaker. In 1845 he published his autobiography, *Narrative of the Life of Frederick Douglass*. The book won great sympathy for the cause of abolition.

In 1850 he said of the Fugitive Slave Act: "Under this law the oaths of any two villains (the capturer and the claimant) are sufficient to confine a free man to slavery for life."

During the Civil War, Douglass recruited blacks for the Union Army and was a trusted advisor to President Lincoln. After the war, Douglass worked to promote the rights of both blacks and women.

❝ I have often been utterly astonished, since I came to the north, to find persons who could speak of the singing, among slaves, as evidence of their contentment and happiness. It is impossible to conceive of a greater mistake. Slaves sing most when they are most unhappy. The songs of the slave represent the sorrows of his heart; and he is relieved by them, only as an aching heart is relieved by its tears. At least, such is my experience. ❞

—from *Narrative of the Life of Frederick Douglass*, 1845

SLAVE NARRATIVES

Slave narratives were the autobiographies of former slaves who had run away, been set free, or otherwise escaped bondage. Abolitionist societies published hundreds of slave narratives in order to win sympathy for the cause; the books helped readers understand the plight of enslaved people. For many northern whites, slave narratives were their first introduction to the idea that blacks were human beings, with actual thoughts and feelings.

Who was the little woman who made a big war?

Seventh child of the famous abolitionist preacher Lyman Beecher, Harriet Beecher Stowe (1811–1896) wrote the novel *Uncle Tom's Cabin* (1852) in reaction to the Fugitive Slave Act. Stowe tried to bring attention to the evils of slavery by telling the stories of families and individuals, including patient and saintly slave Tom. At the end of the novel, Tom is murdered by a cruel overseer.

With more than two million copies printed within five years of publication, *Uncle Tom's Cabin* became the best-selling American novel of the century—and advanced the cause of abolition immeasurably. Upon meeting Stowe at the White House in 1862, Lincoln supposedly said, "So this is the little woman who made this big war!"

Did the Compromise of 1850 work?

The Compromise of 1850 resolved the slavery question just for land won in the Mexican War.

But by the early 1850s, land west of Iowa and Missouri acquired by the Louisiana Purchase was in question. Should slavery be allowed in this new territory or not?

Four times southern congressmen defeated bills that would have organized it as a free territory. Finally, in 1854, Congressman Stephen Douglas proposed the Kansas-Nebraska Act. The act divided the land into two territories: Nebraska to the north and Kansas to the south. Each territory would be allowed to decide for itself whether to allow slavery.

Northerners pointed out, rightly, that the Kansas-Nebraska Act violated the Missouri Compromise of 1820, which said that slavery would not be allowed there. Accordingly, Douglas added language to the Kansas-Nebraska Act that *repealed*, or canceled, the

> **BABY TAD**
>
> After the death of Edward and birth of William (known as Willie) in 1850, Abraham and Mary had one more child—a fourth son, Thomas, in 1853. As an infant Thomas had an unusually large head and skinny body. Abraham thought he looked like a tadpole, and the nickname "Tad" stuck.

Missouri Compromise. With the backing of the Democratic president, Franklin Pierce, Douglas's bill passed through Congress and became law.

Reaction to the Kansas-Nebraska Act varied greatly. Many northerners saw it as a horrible betrayal. Southerners considered it a well-deserved victory.

AMERICAN VOICES

66 The crime is committed. The work of Monroe, and Madison, and Jefferson is undone. The wall they erected to guard the domain of Liberty is flung down by the hands of an American Congress, and Slavery crawls like a slimy reptile over the ruins, to defile a second Eden. 99

—editorial in the Albany, New York, *Evening Journal*, 1854

66 In the South, scarce a ripple seems to agitate the surface of society. All is calmness and equanimity. Here and there we read of resolutions adopted by conventions of the people, or their legislature, but they are distinguished by no mark of intemperance and unnecessary excitement. 99

—editorial in the Jackson, Mississippi, *Mississippian*, 1854

Did Lincoln oppose the Kansas-Nebraska Act?

Lincoln had always believed that slavery was wrong. "Slavery is founded in the selfishness of man's nature," he said. "Opposition to it is his love of justice."

He had long opposed the possibility of slavery in new territories and thought that the Kansas-Nebraska Act was a terrible mistake. He was also appalled by the repeal of Clay's Missouri Compromise. Lincoln's sense of duty now compelled him to reenter politics.

What major political party was born in 1854?

For almost two decades, the dominant American political parties had been the Whigs and the Democrats (see page 29). Several smaller parties formed in the late 1840s and early 1850s, including the Free-Soilers (see page 50) and the Know-Nothings. Originally a secret society, the Know-Nothings (so-called because members claimed they "knew nothing" about the party) protested the many European immigrants flooding to America's shores.

Angered by the Kansas-Nebraska Act, abolitionists formed the Republican Party in 1854. The first Republicans were radical Democrats, Whigs, and Free-Soilers who had given up hope that the established parties would ever oppose slavery strongly enough. The new party was an immediate success. Republicans won forty-four seats in the 1854 congressional elections.

Was Lincoln one of the first Republicans?

At first Lincoln thought the Republicans were too radical, and he opposed certain Free-Soiler elements in the new party. The country's best hope, he still believed, lay with the Whigs.

In 1854 he won a seat in the Illinois state legislature as a Whig, but resigned two weeks later to run for the Senate. Anti-slavery Democrat Lyman Trumbull, whom Lincoln considered to be a good man, won the race instead. As always, Lincoln was good-natured about his defeat. "On the whole, it is perhaps as well for the general cause that Trumbull is elected," he wrote to a friend.

AMERICAN VOICES

66 Our progress in degeneracy appears to me to be pretty rapid. As a nation, we began by declaring that 'all men are created equal.' We now practically read it 'all men are created equal, except negroes.' When the Know-Nothings get control, it will read 'all men are created equal, except negroes and foreigners and Catholics.' When it comes to this, I should prefer emigrating to some country where they make no pretense of loving liberty—to Russia, for instance, where despotism can be taken pure, and without the base alloy of hypocrisy. 99

—**Lincoln**, in an 1855 letter to a friend

Why was Kansas bleeding?

With the passage of the Kansas-Nebraska Act, the two new territories had to settle the question of slavery for themselves. Nebraska was far enough north that there was never any real doubt that it would be free—but things were different in Kansas.

In the early 1850s about fifteen hundred abolitionists from New England had emigrated there to make sure that when the issue was put to the vote, slavery would be defeated. In the South, rumors put the number of new Kansas abolitionists at more than twenty thousand. Proslavery Missourians were alarmed.

In elections in 1854 and 1855, thousands of Missourians poured across the Kansas border and voted, handing races to proslavery candidates. In response, antislavery forces declared the elections illegal and set up an alternative territorial government, which immediately began to campaign for statehood. Confusion reigned.

Violence broke out repeatedly for the next seven years. Homes and businesses were burned. Settlers were shot, hanged, or hacked with knives. The state became known as Bleeding Kansas.

After hundreds of people on both sides died, the proslavery forces were defeated. Kansas became a free state in 1861.

BLEEDING SUMNER

In May 1856 the abolitionist Senator Charles Sumner of Massachusetts delivered a long, passionate speech on the U.S. Senate floor. He condemned proslavery forces in Kansas, calling them "murderous robbers" and "hirelings picked from the drunken spew and vomit of an uneasy civilization," among other things. Sumner also denounced the South generally and referred to the "shameful imbecility" of South Carolina in particular.

Two days later Congressman Preston Brooks of South Carolina approached Sumner at his desk in the Senate. With no warning Brooks began beating Sumner over the head with a gold-handled cane until he lay senseless and bloody.

The incident inflamed the North. "Has it come to this, that we must speak with bated breath in the presence of our Southern masters?" asked William Cullen Bryant, editor of the New York *Post*. "Are we to be chastised as they chastise their slaves?"

Opinion in the South was, not surprisingly, just the opposite: "The vulgar Abolitionists in the Senate . . . have grown saucy, and dare to be impudent to gentlemen! . . . They must be lashed into submission," ran an editorial in the Charleston (South Carolina) *Courier*. Brooks was hailed as a hero and received numerous new canes with mottoes such as "Hit Him Again!" on them.

How did an almanac help Lincoln?

Having lost the Senate election, Lincoln returned to his law office and started to do legal work for railroads, manufacturing companies, and other large businesses.

He didn't always work for big businesses, however. In 1858 the son of his old friend from New Salem days, Jack Armstrong, was accused of murder. With the help of an almanac, Lincoln was able to show that the moon was not out on the night of the crime, and so the eyewitness couldn't have seen Duff Armstrong as was claimed. Lincoln's careful reasoning and eloquent plea for sympathy won the day, and his friend's son was acquitted. Lincoln took no fee for his work on the case.

When did Lincoln become a Republican?

After the Kansas-Nebraska Act was passed, the Whig Party started to fall apart. It had never taken a strong stand on slavery, the issue people in the country cared most about. Lincoln sensed that a new party, taking in the range of antislavery opinion from hard-line abolitionist to discontented Free-Soiler, could succeed.

On May 29, 1856, Lincoln delivered a speech (now known as the "Lost Speech") at the Illinois State Republican Convention, arguing that the various antislavery forces—Whig, Democrat, Free-Soiler, even Know-Nothing—should come together under a single banner. Although supposedly he never used the word *Republican* in his speech (because Republicanism was still considered too radical), Lincoln was now clearly no longer a Whig. He had joined—in fact become a leader of—the Republican Party.

In the fall of 1856, Lincoln compaigned vigorously for the Republican nominee for president, John C. Frémont of New York.

Though he lost to the Democratic candidate, James Buchanan of Pennsylvania, Frémont won a respectable 33 percent of the vote. The Whigs had been unable to mount a campaign at all. Former Whig president Millard Fillmore ran as a Know-Nothing candidate but carried only one state.

The Whig, Free-Soil, and Know-Nothing parties soon faded away, leaving the Republicans and Democrats as the two major American political groups. It's been that way ever since.

THE LOST SPEECH

Several of Lincoln's speeches—the Gettysburg Address, the Second Inaugural—are considered among the greatest in American history. The speech he delivered to the Illinois State Republican Convention, however, may have been his best of all.

William H. Herndon was there and later wrote: "His speech was full of fire and energy and force. It was logic; it was pathos; it was enthusiasm; it was justice, equity, truth, and right set ablaze by the divine fires of a soul maddened by the wrong; it was hard, heavy, knotty, gnarly, backed with wrath."

Lincoln had not prepared the speech beforehand, so there was no written draft of his words. Although there were forty reporters in the audience, he was so mesmerizing that every one of them stopped taking notes in order to listen. Thus perhaps the greatest oration of Lincoln's career was lost forever.

CHAPTER 5

Strong Opinions, Changing Times

Dred Scott

Who compared a man named Dred Scott to a mule?

Dred Scott (1795?–1858), a slave, was taken by his master, John Emerson, from Missouri to the free state of Illinois and then to the free territory of Wisconsin. Scott lived there for four years before returning with Emerson to Missouri. In 1846 Scott sued for his freedom, arguing that his years spent in places where slavery was not allowed had made him a free man.

More than ten years later, in 1857, the case finally made it to the southern-dominated Supreme Court. Chief Justice Roger B. Taney's decision not only said Negroes were not citizens and had no rights but also went even further, declaring that Scott was the property of his owner. This decision meant that an enslaved person was no different from a horse, cow, or mule. Slaves were property, and Congress had no authority to restrict property anywhere in the United States. Further, the court declared the Missouri Compromise unconstitutional: Congress had no power to bar slavery from the territories. In one blow Taney and the other judges had completely knocked down all of the laws Congress had passed to limit or otherwise govern slavery.

The Dred Scott decision outraged the North. And it is now considered to be one of worst decisions ever handed down by the Supreme Court.

Shortly after the case was decided, Dred Scott, his wife, and two daughters were freed by their owners, and he became a porter in a St. Louis hotel. Dred Scott died of tuberculosis in 1858.

What did Lincoln think of the Dred Scott case?

Like many people who disliked slavery, Lincoln hated the Dred Scott decision. He disagreed with it and was disgusted by the idea that people could be considered property in America, where "all men are created equal."

After the decision was made, Lincoln wrote, "[when our nation was founded] our Declaration was held sacred by all, and thought to include all, but now, to aid in making the bondage of the negro universal and eternal, it is assailed and sneered at, and construed, and hawked at, and torn, till, if its framers could rise from their graves, they could not at all recognize it."

The reaction to the decision further split the country. Those who favored slavery, most of them southern Democrats, celebrated the decision because it opened up all the new western territories to slavery.

The new Republican Party was strengthened. Many people who had been sitting on the fence became more opposed to the idea of slavery and were ready to unite in opposition to slavery in the western territories.

A year after the decision, the Illinois Republicans nominated Abraham Lincoln to run against Democrat Stephen Douglas for the U.S. Senate. And on the night of June 16, 1858, Abraham Lincoln stood up to give one of the most important speeches of his life.

How do you divide a house?

Speaking at the Republican convention in June, Lincoln quoted words of Jesus in the Bible and then elaborated upon them: "'A house divided against itself cannot stand.' I believe this government cannot endure permanently half *slave* and half *free*. I do not expect the Union to be dissolved—I do not expect the house to *fall*—but I do expect it will cease to be divided. It will become *all* one thing, or *all* the other." All slave or all free.

Lincoln foresaw the consequences of the Dred Scott decision: If blacks had no rights at all, then what prevented white citizens *anywhere* in the Union—even in the North—from owning them? If slavery could not be banned from the territories, then how could it continue to be banned in some of the states?

"We shall *lie down* pleasantly dreaming that the people of *Missouri* are on the verge of making their State *free*," warned Lincoln; "and we shall *awake* to the *reality*, instead, that the *Supreme* Court has made *Illinois* a *slave* State."

The "House Divided" speech marked another step in Lincoln's long journey toward the abolition of slavery.

What were the Lincoln-Douglas debates?

Lincoln's Democratic opponent for the U.S. Senate was Stephen Douglas, the "Little Giant." The men had known each other over twenty years. During that time Douglas had gained national recognition for the Kansas-Nebraska Act. He was famous for his sharp mind and brilliant speechmaking.

Through the summer of 1858, both Lincoln and Douglas crisscrossed the state of Illinois, speaking at dozens of gatherings large and small. They met up to debate each other in person several times. The debates were staged in little prairie towns in the midsection of the state, where the contest would be decided. (Northern Illinois was solidly Republican, southern Illinois Democratic.) The debates routinely drew crowds of over ten thousand people.

❝I shall have my hands full. He is the strong man of the party—full of wit, facts, dates—and the best stump speaker, with his droll ways and dry jokes, in the West. He is as honest as he is shrewd.**❞**

—**Stephen Douglas**, 1858, on being told that Lincoln would be his opponent

What were the debates like?

Lincoln or Douglas would speak for an hour. His opponent had an hour and a half for rebuttal; and then the opening speaker had half an hour for closing arguments. They took turns opening and closing.

The two men made a striking picture: Lincoln tall and gaunt, raw-boned (but still beardless), in his black stovepipe hat and swallowtail coat, with a high speaking voice that sometimes cracked under the strain of the hot sun. Douglas short and thick, pug faced, shaking his fists like a prizefighter, dressed in frock coat and wide-brimmed white hat, his voice a forceful bark.

Why are the Lincoln-Douglas debates so famous?

Both men were powerful speakers, but what made the debates so important was their unrelenting focus on the Big Question: What to do about slavery?

Lincoln and Douglas race for office in this political cartoon.

As the debates progressed, Lincoln came to emphasize the grievous moral wrong of slavery. Douglas maintained that a territory's decision whether to accept or reject slavery was not a moral issue but merely a matter of majority rule.

Douglas used Lincoln's "House Divided" speech against him. If Lincoln didn't believe the country could go on as it was, was he in favor of breaking up the Union? If not, then how did he propose to eliminate slavery? Was he in favor of abolition?

Lincoln's reply was vague: The end of slavery would come not "in a day, nor in a year, nor in two years. I do not suppose that in a most peaceful way ultimate extinction would occur in less than a hundred years at the least; but that it will occur in the best way for both races in God's good time, I have no doubt."

Repeatedly Douglas accused Lincoln of being in favor of social equality for blacks. Lincoln, he claimed, would grant them the right to vote and sit on juries, allow interracial marriages, and so on. To most whites of the time—even liberal-minded northern whites—these ideas were outlandish and infuriating. Lincoln responded, "I do not understand that because I do not want a negro woman for a slave I must necessarily have her for a wife."

Lincoln argued that Douglas and the Democrats had betrayed the Founding Fathers. While unable to abolish slavery themselves, at least the Founders had recognized that it was wrong. Douglas denied that the Founders believed slavery was wrong: Did Jefferson, author of the Declaration of Independence, "intend to say in that Declaration that his negro slaves, which he held and treated as property, were created his equals by Divine law, and that he was violating the law of God every day of his life by holding them as slaves?"

AMERICAN VOICES

66 I will say then that I am not, nor ever have been, in favor of bringing about in any way the social and political equality of the white and black races—that I am not, nor ever have been, in favor of making voters or jurors of negroes, nor of qualifying them to hold office, nor to intermarry with white people; and I will say in addition to this that there is a physical difference between the white and black races which I believe will forever forbid the two races living together on terms of social and political equality. And inasmuch as they cannot so live, while they do remain together there must be the position of superior and inferior, and I as much as any other man am in favor of having the superior position assigned to the white race. 99

—**Lincoln**, fourth debate with Douglas

Was Lincoln a racist in 1858?

By the standards of our day, the answer is yes.

During the first debate with Douglas, Lincoln said, "[A black man] is not my equal in many respects, certainly not in color—perhaps not in intellectual and moral endowments; but in the right to eat the bread without leave of anybody else which his own hand earns, he is my equal."

Lincoln believed the ideal solution to the problem of race in America was for blacks to resettle in another country. There they could enjoy the basic rights to which they were entitled. He feared that blacks, as a minority, would never win full civil rights in the United States.

That Lincoln expressed racist sentiments can't be denied. However, it shouldn't be forgotten that, as a politician, he couldn't afford to appear to be much more progressive than voters on matters of race. At that time the voting public was entirely white and male and overwhelmingly racist in its views.

AMERICAN VOICES

66 Viewed from the genuine abolition ground, Mr. Lincoln seemed tardy, cold and indifferent, but measuring him by the sentiment of his country, a sentiment he was bound as a statesman to consult, he was swift, zealous, radical and determined. 99

—**Frederick Douglass**, 1876

Who won the Lincoln-Douglas debates?

At the time, reaction was mixed. Each man's supporters claimed their candidate had utterly crushed the other. Objective observers (if there were any) probably would have called each man a winner.

Douglas was a winner because the Democrats won more seats in the state legislature, and so he was reelected to the U.S. Senate. But Lincoln emerged a winner too. The debates had drawn coverage from national newspapers and magazines. Lincoln had taken on the famous Little Giant and fought him to a standstill. The lanky Illinois lawyer was now one of the most famous Republicans in the nation.

AMERICAN VOICES

❝ It was then and there [Lincoln] told me that, when he was clerking in a country store, his highest political ambition was to be a member of the state Legislature. 'Since then, of course,' he said laughingly, 'I have grown some. . . . I did not consider myself qualified for the United States Senate, and it took me a long time to persuade myself that I was. Now, to be sure,' he continued, with another of his peculiar laughs, 'I am convinced that I am good enough for it; but, in spite of it all, I am saying to myself every day: "It is too big a thing for you; you will never get it." Mary . . . insists, however, that I am going to be Senator and President of the United States, too.' These last words he followed with a roar of laughter, with his arms around his knees, and shaking all over with mirth at his wife's ambition. 'Just think,' he exclaimed, 'of such a sucker as me as President!' ❞

—**Henry Villard**, from "Recollections of Lincoln," 1904. Villard was a journalist who covered the Lincoln-Douglas debates.

Who was John Brown?

Born in Connecticut in 1800, John Brown was among the abolitionists who moved to Kansas after the Kansas-Nebraska Act was passed (see page 63). There Brown and several of his sons murdered five proslavery men. Forced to go into hiding, the Browns eventually settled in Maryland, where they started training a small army of militant abolitionists. In October 1859 Brown led about twenty men, including three of his sons, on a raid on the arsenal at Harpers Ferry, Virginia (now West Virginia). The plan was to capture the weapons stored in  the arsenal and to use those weapons to raise a slave revolt that would sweep through the South.

Brown's men were trapped in the arsenal by angry, gun-toting townspeople. Shots were exchanged, and men on both sides fell. Two days after the fighting began, federal forces led by Colonel Robert E. Lee stormed the arsenal. About half of Brown's men were killed, including two of his sons. Brown himself was wounded by a sword and taken prisoner. He was charged with treason and hanged six weeks later.

WHAT DOES IT MEAN?

During the Revolutionary War, a *Yankee* was any American. By the time of the Civil War, *Yankee* had come to mean anyone from the northern states.

Northern abolitionists regarded Brown as a hero and martyr. "No man in America has ever stood up so persistently and effectively for the dignity of human nature," said the great Yankee writer Henry David Thoreau.

Southerners considered Brown a demon and a madman, so crazed he was hardly responsible for his actions. As one Harpers Ferry resident said, "What else could be expected from him, or anyone else who are imbued with 'Freeloveism, Socialism, Spiritualism,' and all the other isms that were ever devised by man or devil."

AMERICAN VOICES

❝ I, John Brown, am now quite certain that the crimes of this guilty land will never be purged away but with blood. ❞

—John Brown's prophetic warning, scrawled on a piece of paper just moments before his hanging

What was the Cooper Union Address?

In February 1860 Lincoln spoke at Cooper Institute in Manhattan.

He argued that Republicans were conservative, not radical and divisive as many southerners and Democrats claimed. It was the South that wanted to overturn eighty years of limited slavery; Republicans were happy to leave the South alone, as long as slavery was limited to it.

In response to the charge that Republicans encouraged slave revolts, Lincoln remarked: "John Brown was no Republican; and you have failed to implicate a single Republican in his Harpers Ferry enterprise."

Lincoln concluded, "Neither let us be slandered from our duty by false accusations against us, nor frightened from it by menaces of destruction to the Government nor of dungeons to ourselves. *Let us have faith that right makes might, and in that faith let us, to the end, dare to do our duty as we understand it.*"

What became known as the Cooper Union Address was a resounding success. The speech was reprinted in full in newspapers across the North. Lincoln's star rose ever higher. In May, at the Republican National Convention in Chicago, he was chosen as the presidential candidate. He would square off once again against his old nemesis, the Little Giant, Stephen Douglas.

AMERICAN VOICES

❝ When Lincoln rose to speak, I was greatly disappointed. He was tall, tall,—oh, how tall! and so angular and awkward that I had, for an instant, a feeling of pity for so ungainly a man. ❞
—one eyewitness to the Cooper Union Address, as quoted in *Lincoln's Yarns & Stories*, by Colonel Alexander K. McClure, 1901

What helped Lincoln win?

In some ways Lincoln's lack of experience in office worked to his advantage: he had little public record to defend. He ran largely on his personal qualities—his gift for oratory, his reputation for honesty, his wondrous life story. Even in those days, the log-cabin imagery of his frontier youth held romantic appeal. "Honest Abe, the Rail-Splitter" he was called in campaign pamphlets and posters.

Republican Party leaders who had lost the nomination swallowed their disappointment and campaigned for Lincoln and his running mate, Hannibal Hamlin of Maine.

In contrast, the opposition was divided. Stephen Douglas, John C. Breckinridge, and John Bell received almost a million more votes than Lincoln, who wasn't even on the southern states' ballots. Still, Lincoln won all the northern states except New Jersey, which he split with Douglas. The northern vote was enough to give Lincoln the election.

Lincoln was often called the "rail candidate."

How did the South react to Lincoln's election?

Outrage! "The election of Abraham Lincoln has put the country in peril," claimed an editorial in the *Richmond Dispatch*. Southern leaders understood, correctly, that Lincoln had been elected by the North. That the North would choose a man so distasteful to the South proved that the two regions could no longer get along. The Union could hold no longer.

WHAT DOES IT MEAN?

A *confederacy* is a loose grouping or league.

On December 20, South Carolina *seceded*, or withdrew, from the United States. Mississippi, Florida, Alabama, Georgia, Louisiana, and Texas soon followed. The rebel states began organizing themselves into a new nation, the Confederate States of America. By the time Lincoln reached Washington for his inauguration in March 1861, Jefferson Davis of Mississippi had already been named the president of the Confederacy.

❝ [The Republican Party has established an] absolute tyranny over the slaveholding States. And all without the smallest warrant, excuse or justification. We have appealed to their generosity, justice and patriotism, but all without avail. . . . They have robbed us of our property. . . . ❞

—*New Orleans Daily Crescent*, in response to Lincoln's election

"ALL THE LADIES LIKE WHISKERS"

Until 1860 Lincoln had gone clean shaven his whole life. In October, just before the election, he received the following letter:

Dear Sir

My father has just come from the fair and brought home your picture and Mr. Hamlin's. I am a little girl only 11 years old, but want you should be President of the United States very much so I hope you wont think me very bold to write to such a great man as you are. Have you any little girls about as large as I am if so give them my love and tell her to write to me . . . . I have got 4 brother's and part of them will vote for you any way and if you let your whiskers grow I will try and get the rest of them to vote for you you would look a great deal better for your face is so thin. All the ladies like whiskers and they would tease their husband's to vote for you and then you would be President. . . .

Good bye

Grace Bedell

In his reply Lincoln asked Grace, "As to the whiskers, having never worn any, do you not think people would call it a piece of silly affection [*sic*] if I were to begin it now?"

Silly affectation or not, Lincoln grew out his whiskers. He thanked Grace Bedell personally for her good advice when his train stopped in her hometown the following February.

Was Lincoln welcomed in Washington?

(3.) THE SPECIAL TRAIN
" He wore a Scotch plaid Cap and a very long Military Cloak, so that he was entirely unrecognizable."

This *Harper's Weekly* cartoon depicts a disguised Lincoln fleeing potential assassins.

Rumors of an assassination attempt dogged the family's train journey east to Washington. When the Lincolns arrived in the capital, they found that much of Washington society and the press looked down on them. The Lincolns were pictured as country bumpkins who didn't know which fork to use. One news story reported that Lincoln had snuck into the city in a disguise. His enemies in the North called him a coward. Southerners called him much worse.

What did Lincoln say in his First Inaugural Address?

The importance of preserving the Union was the one and only subject of his First Inaugural Address on March 4, 1861. He hoped against hope that the secession crisis would blow over—that the southern states would voluntarily return to the Union. To persuade them to come back, he offered the proverbial carrot and stick.

The carrot was his promise that he wouldn't interfere with southerners' right to hold slaves.

The stick was his threat that "all the powers at my disposal will be used to reclaim the public property and places which have fallen." However, he also said, "the government will not assail *you*, unless *you* first assail it."

In closing, he appealed to southerners' patriotic feelings in words that have become some of his most memorable: "We are not enemies, but friends. We must not be enemies. Though passion may have strained, it must not break our bonds of affection. The mystic chords of memory, stretching from every battle-field, and patriot grave, to every living heart and hearthstone, all over this broad land, will yet swell the chorus of the Union, when again touched, as surely they will be, by the better angels of our nature."

His speech fell on deaf ears. Within six weeks war would break out and four more states would secede.

What Became of the Little Giant?

In the months immediately following the election, Stephen Douglas put away any bitterness he might have felt and worked to keep the country together. When war broke out, he offered his services to Lincoln, but unfortunately, he died of typhoid fever just months later. In his last words, he left advice for his sons to "obey the laws and support the Constitution of the United States."

CHAPTER 6

Johnny Reb and Billy Yank

Bombardment of Fort Sumter

What was the first clash of war?

Fort Sumter, in the harbor of Charleston, South Carolina, was held by troops loyal to the Union. In January 1861 Confederate forces surrounded the fort, preventing food supplies from getting through. On April 11 the Confederate general P.G.T. Beauregard demanded that the fort be turned over to his men. The Union commander, Major Robert Anderson, refused to surrender. The next day Beauregard ordered an assault on the fort.

For thirty hours the Confederates lobbed mortar shells at the fort. The ninety Union soldiers inside—surrounded, outnumbered, tired, and hungry—never had a chance. On April 14 Anderson and his men gave up. Beauregard allowed them to board a ship headed to New York. Remarkably, there were no casualties during the first clash of the Civil War.

The next day Lincoln called for seventy-five thousand volunteers to enlist in the army. Within days Virginia left the Union and joined the Confederacy. Three more states would follow.

CONFEDERACY STATES AND DATES OF SECESSION
South Carolina—December 20, 1860
Mississippi—January 9, 1861
Florida—January 10, 1861
Alabama—January 11, 1861
Georgia—January 19, 1861
Louisiana—January 26, 1861
Texas—February 1, 1861
Virginia—April 17, 1861
Arkansas—May 6, 1861
North Carolina—May 20, 1861
Tennessee—June 8, 1861

What were the border states?

The slave states of Kentucky and Missouri had pro-Confederate and pro-Union sympathizers in late 1861. Each state was admitted to the Confederacy under its pro-Confederate government, though each state also remained in the Union under its pro-Union government. Slavery was legal in Delaware and Maryland, but like Kentucky and Missouri, they stayed in the Union.

These four states—Kentucky, Missouri, Delaware, and Maryland—were known as the *border states*. Lincoln believed that keeping them in the Union was crucial to the war effort.

In each of the border states, loyalties were torn. Here the Civil War stories of brother fighting brother, and father fighting son, rang most true.

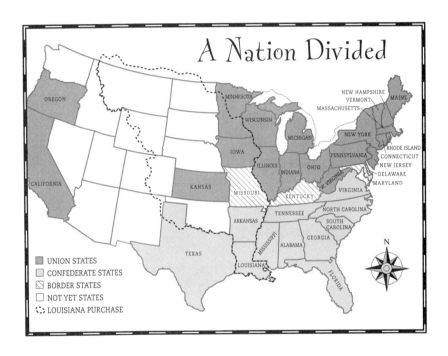

A Nation Divided

UNION STATES
CONFEDERATE STATES
BORDER STATES
NOT YET STATES
LOUISIANA PURCHASE

What new state was born out of war?

Enslaved people had worked on farms and plantations in Virginia since before the Revolution. But the northwest section of the state, cut off by mountains from the rest of Virginia, had been pioneered by people who did not own slaves. These people did not want to leave the Union.

In June 1861, only two months after Virginia seceded, leaders from some of these northwestern counties met in Wheeling to secede from the rest of Virginia. Two years later, West Virginia was admitted to the Union as the thirty-fifth state.

Who was the Sphinx?

Jefferson Davis, president of the Confederacy

One of the first things the new Confederate States of America had to do was choose its own president. Jefferson Davis, who had been a senator from Mississippi, was chosen to lead the new "country" by a group of representatives from the Confederacy. He was later elected by popular vote.

Like Lincoln, Jefferson Davis (1808–1889) was born in a log cabin on the Kentucky frontier. But that is about all their boyhoods had in common. Davis's family soon moved south to Mississippi, where they prospered. He graduated from West Point as an officer in the U.S. Army in 1828.

Davis saw real action in the Black Hawk War. In the Mexican War, he was wounded at the Battle of Buena Vista. Davis returned to Mississippi a hero and was elected to the Senate. In 1853 he was named war secretary by President Franklin Pierce and was responsible for modernizing and reorganizing the U.S. Army.

Davis later returned to the Senate and even thought of running for president in 1860. But when Mississippi seceded from the Union, Davis resigned. Although he wanted to serve in the Confederate military, Davis was asked to lead the new government.

The job he took on was not going to be easy, and his personality didn't help. Jefferson Davis was distant and cold; he was known as "the Sphinx" because his face had so little expression.

AMERICAN VOICES

❝ My own convictions as to negro slavery are strong. It has its evils and abuses. . . . We recognize the negro as God and God's Book and God's Laws in Nature tell us to recognize him—our inferior fitted expressly for servitude. You cannot transform the negro into anything one-tenth as useful or good as what slavery enables them to be. ❞

—**Jefferson Davis**, after his election

FIRST LADY OF THE CONFEDERACY

Varina Howell (1826–1906) of Natchez, Mississippi, was just eighteen when she married the thirty-six-year-old Jefferson Davis and twenty when he entered Congress. Varina Davis was no meek political wife, however. She was well educated and held her own opinions—against secession, for example—and she wasn't afraid to express them.

Did Americans admire the Union's First Lady?

The Lincolns' country-bumpkin image never bothered Abraham much, but it troubled Mary Todd Lincoln.

When it became known that much of the Todd family had sided with the South—three of Mary's half-brothers and her brother-in-law, Ben Hardin Helm, eventually bore arms for the Confederacy—rumors began circulating that Mary herself was a southern sympathizer, even a spy. The charge was untrue, of course. Ironically, she was denounced as a traitor in the South as well.

Mary Lincoln liked to go on shopping sprees, taking trips to Philadelphia and New York to buy fashionable clothes. She redecorated the White House with expensive furniture, spending more money than Congress had given her. Newspapers attacked her for spending so much, especially since the nation was at war.

Washington high society thought little of the First Lady, and some of the White House staff even gave her the nickname "Hellcat." One British journalist expressed his contempt in this 1862 letter to a friend: "Did you cast your eye over the acc[ount] of Mrs. Lincoln's Ball? Was there ever such snobbery & ridiculous sickening trash? She's like a damned old Irish or Scotch (or English) washerwoman dressed out for a Sunday."

How was life at the White House for the Lincoln boys?

Robert was a student at Harvard University when the Lincolns moved to Washington, but Willie was only eleven and Tad was nearly eight. The younger boys soon had a small zoo—cats, dogs, goats, rabbits, ponies—and they kept the staff busy with their mischief. They even turned one section of the White House's flat roof into a ship's deck, complete with rigging.

The boys were tutored at home. Willie was a quick and gifted student. Tad "had a very bad opinion of books and no opinion of discipline," according to one of Lincoln's private secretaries, John Hay.

Willie and Tad played lots of army games. Sometimes their father played along. Once the boys let it be known that a favorite soldier doll had been court-martialed for sleeping on duty—a capital offense. Before they had a chance to carry out the death sentence, they received a surprise note on executive mansion stationery: "The doll Jack is pardoned. By order of the President. A. Lincoln."

What does a snake have to do with war?

Most people believed that the war would be over in a few months. The first commander of the Union armies, General Winfield Scott, planned to force the Confederacy to surrender by using the superior Union navy to blockade southern ports. He would then take control of the Mississippi River. The main supply routes of the South would be cut off, and the Confederacy would slowly be squeezed to death. Then Union troops could capture Richmond,

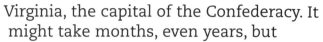

Virginia, the capital of the Confederacy. It might take months, even years, but eventually the Confederacy would succumb to Scott's "Anaconda Plan," named for the large snake that squeezes its prey to death.

Lincoln hoped for a quicker end to the war. Newspapers in the North mocked Scott's plan and demanded action.

What happened at Bull Run?

In July Union General Irvin McDowell led thirty-five thousand green recruits toward Richmond. On July 21, 1861, McDowell's men met twenty-two thousand Confederates under the command of General P.G.T. Beauregard at a stream called Bull Run near the town of Manassas Junction, Virginia. It was the first major battle of the Civil War.

Though the Confederate rebels were outnumbered, they held firm against Union assault. Then Confederate General Joseph E. Johnston arrived with nine thousand men and turned back the Union troops, who retreated to Washington in disarray.

While the Union resolved to gain revenge for the humiliating defeat, the Confederates rejoiced over their victory. But both sides came to the terrible realization that the war would not end quickly or painlessly. At First Bull Run—also known as First

Manassas—about twenty-nine hundred Union soldiers were killed, wounded, or captured. The Confederacy lost almost two thousand soldiers.

A little more than a year later, in August 1862, Union and Confederate troops clashed again at the same place. The Second Battle of Bull Run, also known as the Battle of Second Manassas, was an overwhelming victory for the Confederacy.

Bull Run v. Manassas

The engagement was known as the Battle of Bull Run (after the nearby stream) in the Union, and as the Battle of Manassas (after the nearby town) in the Confederacy. Both names are valid. Several other major Civil War battles have more than one name, including:

Union / Confederate

Pittsburg Landing = Shiloh, TN

Antietam = Sharpsburg, MD

Stones River = Murfreesboro, TN

Opequon Creek = Winchester, VA

Who fought the Civil War?

In the armies of both sides, men of every age and from every walk of life filled the ranks. Officers, who had to be able to read and write orders, were generally drawn from the educated classes. Many privates were unschooled laborers—farmworkers, miners, factory workers.

At first both armies were composed entirely of volunteers. But as the war dragged on, fewer men were willing to join. Both sides resorted to *conscription*, or a military draft. That meant both governments required men to fight. The mere threat of the draft was often enough to inspire working-class men to sign up, since you were paid a bonus to volunteer. If you were going to go into the army anyway, it was better to get paid than not.

In both the Union and Confederate states, rich men were able to buy their way out of service by hiring a substitute. Substitutes were generally young men with little money and few prospects who weren't, for whatever reason, subject to the draft. If a substitute couldn't be found, rich men could *commute*, or cancel, their service by simply paying the government a large fee.

The practices of substitution and commutation led to the angry slogan "Rich man's war, poor man's fight." It was a cry heard in both the Union and the Confederacy.

Who fought in the War?

It's called the Civil War in some places, the War Between the States in others. It's sometimes called the War Between North and South.

The armies of the Union, whose soldiers were nicknamed "Billy Yank," mostly came from the northern states. But more than three hundred thousand southerners remained loyal to the Union during the war. While their uniforms were typically blue, every state had its own colorful uniforms.

The soldiers of the Confederacy were known as "Johnny Reb." Most of them were poor, young workingmen and farm boys from the southern states. Although "cadet gray" was selected as the color of their uniforms, each Confederate state had different-colored uniforms, some of them brown or butternut (a light brownish gray). And many soldiers had no uniforms at all. They wore their own clothes into battle. Sometimes Confederate units wore blue uniforms taken from dead and captured Union soldiers. Unfortunately, this often meant confusion on the battlefield, where all the different uniforms made it hard to tell which side a man was on.

Did blacks also fight?

Free black men had served in every American war since the Revolution. But the idea of black soldiers was not a popular one. Many people on both sides were afraid to give blacks guns, fearing that they might rebel and turn on whites. Lincoln himself opposed the idea of allowing blacks to fight; he was afraid it would frighten people in the four border states and cause great resistance to the Union cause. He also thought it would inflame the people in the Confederacy, making them fight even harder.

But from the early days of the war, blacks served in Union armies, often as cooks or laborers. And some Union generals, who were eager to have all able-bodied men they could get their hands on, wanted to recruit blacks as soldiers.

As the fighting went on, it became clear that the war's outcome would decide the fate of black people in America. The Union navy had accepted men of all colors from the very outset of the war. In 1862 Congress allowed blacks to enroll in the army for war service. The first black units were formed of free blacks and freed slaves who had been "confiscated" from their owners, although the Union government did not officially recognize the units yet. After the Emancipation Proclamation in 1863, the enlistment of blacks became Union policy.

The first officially recognized all-black units were the 54th and 55th Massachusetts. (The story of the 54th Massachusetts Infantry is told in the excellent film *Glory*.) As the Union armies captured more southern territory, more slaves escaped their owners and joined the Union fight. Eventually more than two hundred thousand blacks served in the Union cause.

At the end of the war, the Confederate government, desperate to fill its ranks, also allowed blacks to enlist, but few did. Earlier in the war, many black slaves had gone to war as servants to their Confederate masters.

❝ No officer in this regiment now doubts that the key to the successful prosecution of this war lies in the unlimited employment of black troops. Their superiority lies simply in the fact that they know the country, while white troops do not, and, moreover, that they have peculiarities of temperament, position, and motive which belong to them alone. Instead of leaving their homes and families to fight they are fighting for their homes and families, and they show the resolution and sagacity which a personal purpose gives. **❞**

—from a report by Colonel **Thomas Wentworth Higginson**, commander of the First South Carolina Volunteer Infantry, Colored, February 1, 1863

Where was the Civil War fought?

More battles by far took place in Virginia than in any other state or territory, but there were skirmishes all over the South and even in such northern locales as Ohio and Indiana. Fighting also occurred as far west as Missouri, Arkansas, and Texas.

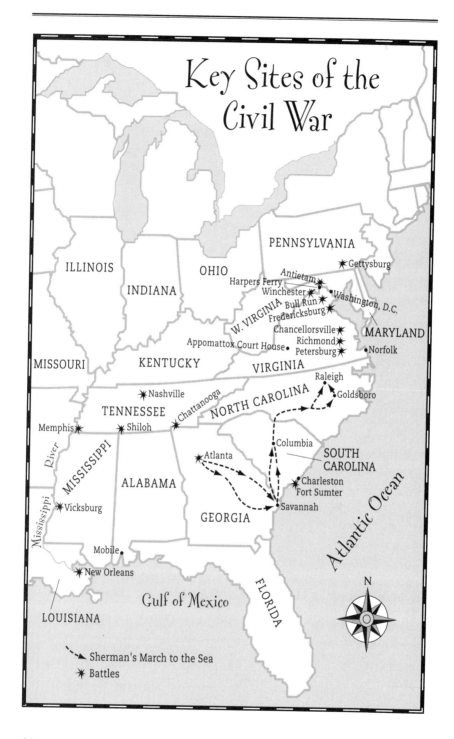

Key Sites of the Civil War

ILLINOIS

INDIANA

OHIO

PENNSYLVANIA

★ Gettysburg

Antietam ★
Harpers Ferry ★
Winchester ★ Washington, D.C.
Bull Run ★
Fredericksburg ★
Chancellorsville ★
Appomattox Court House · Richmond ★
Petersburg ★
Norfolk ·

W. VIRGINIA

MARYLAND

MISSOURI

KENTUCKY

VIRGINIA

TENNESSEE

★ Nashville

Chattanooga ·

NORTH CAROLINA

Raleigh ·
· Goldsboro

Memphis ★

★ Shiloh

Columbia ·

SOUTH
CAROLINA

★ Atlanta

MISSISSIPPI

ALABAMA

· Charleston
Fort Sumter

★ Vicksburg

GEORGIA

Savannah ·

Atlantic Ocean

Mobile ·

Mississippi River

★ New Orleans

FLORIDA

Gulf of Mexico

N

LOUISIANA

- → Sherman's March to the Sea
★ Battles

Why did Lincoln go through so many generals?

During the first half of the war, Lincoln had no luck finding an effective commander for the Army of the Potomac (the main Union force in the East).

General Winfield Scott (1786–1866), a hero of the Mexican War, was the ranking Union general at the start of the Civil War. He retired shortly after First Bull Run.

Scott's successor, General George B. McClellan (1826–1885), was called "the Virginia Creeper" because he was so reluctant to attack. Lincoln once remarked, "If McClellan is not using the army, I should like to borrow it for a while." By November 1862 he had lost patience with McClellan's dithering and fired him.

General Ambrose E. Burnside (1824–1881) gained fame not for his battlefield prowess but for his distinctive facial hair—the word *sideburn* was coined as a play on his name. A friendly and popular fellow, Burnside lost several battles before Lincoln replaced him.

Burnside's successor, General Joseph Hooker (1814–1879), was an ambitious, womanizing boozer who promised immediate success. But after the Union suffered a terrible whipping at the Battle of Chancellorsville (Virginia), Hooker resigned.

Lincoln replaced Hooker with General George Gordon Meade (1815–1872), hoping he was the general the army so badly needed.

Who was the South's favorite son?

General Robert E. Lee (1807–1870) was admired and loved—even worshipped—in a way that Jefferson Davis never was.

Lee was born into one of Virginia's most prominent families. His father, "Lighthorse Harry" Lee, had delivered George Washington's eulogy, and his wife, Mary Custis Lee, was Martha Washington's great-granddaughter. Robert E. Lee finished second in his class at West Point and served honorably under General Winfield Scott in the Mexican War.

Lincoln, recognizing Lee's genius, offered him command of the Union army at the start of the war. Lee refused. No great supporter of slavery (though his extended family did own hundreds of slaves), he felt more loyalty to Virginia than he did to the Union.

After a slow start, Lee began winning battles, including Fredericksburg (over Burnside) and Chancellorsville (over Hooker). The South continued to view him as faultless—even godlike—till the very end.

After the war, Lee became president of Washington College (now Washington and Lee University) in Virginia.

66 It is well that war is so terrible—we should grow too fond of it. **99**
—**Robert E. Lee** at the Battle of Fredericksburg, December 1862

WHAT CONFEDERATE GENERAL STOOD "LIKE A STONE WALL"?

Thomas J. "Stonewall" Jackson (1824–1863) of Virginia earned his nickname at First Bull Run, when he and his men refused to budge under Union attack. Jackson fought with Lee during the defense of Richmond in 1862 and led troops at Second Bull Run, Antietam, Fredericksburg, and Chancellorsville, where he was mortally wounded by friendly fire. Along with Lee, Jackson became one of the major southern heroes of the Civil War.

Where was the Union most successful?

While Lincoln struggled with the command in the East, Union Major General Ulysses S. Grant scored a major victory at Shiloh, Tennessee, April 1862. Within weeks the Union took control of the Confederate railway system centered at Corinth, Mississippi. Then the city of Memphis, Tennessee, fell to the Union. Meanwhile, Union Admiral David Glasgow Farragut was leading a naval force up the Mississippi delta and capturing New Orleans, the South's largest city. In four months the Union seized fifty thousand square miles of territory.

What did other countries think of the Civil War?

From the summer of 1861, Union warships patrolled the waters outside such major southern ports as Norfolk, Virginia; Charleston, South Carolina; Savannah, Georgia; Mobile, Alabama; and New Orleans, Louisiana. Over time this blockade hurt the South's ability to buy things it needed, such as ammunition and medicine, and to sell its main export, cotton.

Three quarters of Britain's cotton came from the American South, and Britain wasn't happy about having its cotton supply (not to mention its market for ammunition and other supplies) dry up. Neither was France.

Jefferson Davis hoped these countries would send ships to break up the blockade. However, as the war progressed, it became clear that the corn and wheat shipped from the North were at least as important to Britain and France as the cotton produced in the South. King Corn defeated King Cotton.

What tragedy befell the Lincolns in early 1862?

In February the Lincolns' beloved eleven-year-old son, Willie, died, probably of typhoid fever.

Well behaved, studious, mature beyond his years, Willie was said to have been, of all the Lincoln children, the most like his father. Abraham was deeply saddened by the loss. He said, "My poor boy. He was too good for this earth. God has called him home. I know that he is much better off in heaven, but then we loved him so. It is hard, hard to have him die."

❝ In this sad world of ours, sorrow comes to all; and, to the young, it comes with bitterest agony, because it takes them unawares. The older have learned to ever expect it. I am anxious to afford some alleviation of your present distress. Perfect relief is not possible, except with time. You cannot now realize that you will ever feel better. Is not this so? And yet it is a mistake. You are sure to be happy again. To know this, which is certainly true, will make you some less miserable now. I have had experience enough to know what I say; and you need only to believe it, to feel better at once. ❞

—**Abraham Lincoln**, in a letter written later that same year to a family friend whose father had died

How did Willie's death affect Mary?

As president, Lincoln couldn't afford to grieve openly for too long. However, Mary was inconsolable. She sought comfort in "spiritualists" (con artists similar to today's "psychics") who claimed to be able to speak to her son from beyond the grave.

For a year Mary rarely left the White House, yet she never entered the room where Willie had died. The press no longer scorned her extravagant entertaining. Now she was accused of shirking her duties as First Lady!

Though Mary acted more and more irrationally, Abraham stood by her. "My wife is as handsome as when she was a girl and I . . . fell in love with her," he said, "and what is more, I have never fallen out."

What important piece of legislation did Lincoln sign in 1862?

Many northerners had long been urging the government to give land in the territories to settlers. Southerners had opposed the giveaway, fearing (correctly) that the western territories would fill up with independent farmers who didn't own slaves.

With the war, there was no longer any southern opposition in Congress to the land giveaway. As a former Whig, Lincoln believed wholeheartedly in government measures that would improve land and increase economic opportunity. In May 1862 he signed the Homestead Act into law.

Under the act, almost anyone who hadn't borne arms against the Union—including former slaves and women—could claim 160 acres of undeveloped public land. If the person built a house on the land, farmed it, and lived on it for five years, the land was theirs. These new settlers spelled disaster for the Indians, whose lifestyle depended in large part on open land and freely roaming buffalo.

Between 1862 and 1976, when the act was repealed, over 270 million acres—10 percent of the entire United States—had been claimed. Today nearly one out of every four American adults owns wealth that can be traced to the Homestead Act. It was one of the most important pieces of legislation ever passed in the history of the nation.

How did Lincoln feel about the fate of the Indians?

In 1862 a group of Santee Sioux Indians in Minnesota, angered by their mistreatment at the hands of whites, rose up and killed over six hundred soldiers, settlers, and traders. Within weeks the Minnesota Uprising (also known as the Dakota Conflict) was quashed by the U.S. Army. A large number of Santee were put on trial for murder. Each trial took, on average, less than ten minutes. The courts found more than three hundred Santees guilty and sentenced them to death.

When Lincoln reviewed the trial transcripts, he realized that most of the Indians had been convicted not for their actions, but merely because they were Santee. He canceled the death sentences of all but thirty-nine of the men—the greatest single act of clemency by a president. Still, the mass execution that followed was the largest in American history.

Lincoln believed Indians would have to give up their traditional lifestyles and *assimilate*, or blend in, with the white majority. In 1863 he met with leaders of several major tribes. He praised them for the way their people lived in harmony with the land; nevertheless, he told the Indians that they should settle down and become farmers.

Did the Emancipation Proclamation free the slaves?

As the war progressed, Lincoln came to understand that the South would have to be punished and permanently weakened. Public opinion in the North was growing ever more inclined toward abolition.

This statue of Lincoln freeing a slave is displayed in Washington, D.C.'s Lincoln Park.

Opposing slavery on moral grounds, Lincoln now saw that abolition was becoming a political necessity. Through the spring of 1862, he pleaded with the border states to adopt some form of abolition with *restitution*. (That is, former slave owners would be paid by the federal government for their loss of "property.") The border states wouldn't budge.

With Union losses in the East mounting, Lincoln realized that a bold stroke—one that would both weaken the South and galvanize the North— was necessary. In July 1862 he decided what that stroke would be. He waited until September 22, four days after the Union victory at Antietam, Maryland, to issue the preliminary Emancipation Proclamation. It said that as of January 1, 1863, all slaves in any state still in rebellion—excepting certain parts of certain states—would be free. States *not* in rebellion were not affected by the proclamation.

Therefore the preliminary Emancipation Proclamation did not free any of the slaves in the border states. Lincoln didn't want to risk pushing these states into the Confederacy by freeing their slaves. For the same reason, the proclamation did not free the slaves in certain counties in Virginia and Louisiana that were under federal control and no longer in rebellion. In fact, the preliminary Emancipation Proclamation left the door open for no slaves to be freed, if the rebellious states returned to the Union before the following January. Of course, no southern state took Lincoln up on his offer.

When January 1, 1863, arrived, the final Emancipation Proclamation went into effect. But just because Lincoln proclaimed slaves in the Confederacy free didn't make them so; southern slaveholders didn't exactly go around telling slaves they had been liberated. Word of the proclamation took months to reach some parts of the Deep South. It would be up to the Union army to enforce the new decree.

> **WHAT DOES IT MEAN?**
>
> An *emancipation* is an act of setting free.
>
> A *proclamation* is a statement or announcement.

Were abolitionists overjoyed by the Emancipation Proclamation?

Many were happy, but a large number of radical Republicans were displeased that the slaves of the border states remained in bondage. They felt that Lincoln had once again not gone far enough. His own secretary of state, William Seward, said, "We show our sympathy with slavery by emancipating slaves where we cannot reach them and holding them in bondage where we can set them free."

One important abolitionist who always supported Lincoln was Frederick Douglass. Though he was frustrated at times by Lincoln's slowness to take up abolitionism, Douglass always believed that his people's best hope lay with Lincoln. And despite Lincoln's occasional public utterances to the contrary, Douglass believed him to be free of racism.

After Lincoln's death Douglass wrote, "I was impressed with his entire freedom from popular prejudice against the colored race. He was the first great man that I talked with in the United States freely, who in no single instance reminded me of the difference between himself and myself."

AMERICAN VOICES

66 The fiery trial through which we pass, will light us down, in honor or dishonor, to the latest generation. . . . In *giving* freedom to the *slave*, we *assure* freedom to the *free*—honorable alike in what we give, and what we preserve. We shall nobly save, or meanly lose, the last best hope of earth. 99
—from Lincoln's State of the Union Address, December 1, 1862

CHAPTER 7

A New Birth of Freedom

Lincoln reads to his youngest son, Tad.

What was a typical day like for President Lincoln?

Lincoln usually got up before seven, put in an hour of work, then had a light breakfast of an egg and coffee. After another hour or two of reading reports and writing letters, he met with visitors—mostly cabinet members, senators, and representatives—until early afternoon. He tried to avoid army officers, who usually were just looking for promotions.

Lincoln liked to see ordinary citizens, but it wasn't always possible.

Many of the citizens he met with were mothers or wives who had come to plead for a young soldier's life or freedom. Desertion and dereliction of duty, such as falling asleep while on watch, were punishable by imprisonment, even death.

Lincoln is known to have taken pity on countless young men and spared their lives. "Let this woman have her son out of Old Capital Prison," and similar notes brought joy to the petitioner and, no doubt, a form of peace to the president as well.

Afternoons were spent signing army commissions and reviewing other military matters. As executive in chief, Lincoln was also the head of the State Department, the Interior Department, and the Justice Department. He had to go through the many reports—recommendations and disputes—generated by various federal agencies.

At four Lincoln would go for a carriage ride with Mary, sometimes visiting wounded soldiers, both Union and Confederate, in local hospitals.

The Lincolns ate dinner at six, usually a simple meal of meat and potatoes. Once a week, during the winter, Lincoln would shake hands and greet folks after dinner. He attended evening concerts and the theater when his schedule permitted. Sometimes he would play with Tad or read to him. Otherwise it was back to work in his office for several more hours, with a late-evening visit to the War Department telegraph office his final chore of the day.

Wartime Humor

Many of Lincoln's day-to-day orders showed that, even during wartime, he hadn't lost his sense of humor.

In response to a young woman's plea on behalf of her husband: "Please have the adjutant general ascertain whether second Lieutenant of Company D, 2nd infantry, Alexander E. Drake, is entitled to promotion. His wife thinks he is. Please have this looked into."

On the papers of a man who'd deserted and then attempted to reenlist and collect another bonus: "Let him fight, instead of shooting him."

To a man who'd come to ask for a job: "This man wants to work, so uncommon a want that I think it ought to be gratified."

AMERICAN VOICES

66 If you once forfeit the confidence of your fellow citizens, you can never regain their respect and esteem. It is true that you may fool all the people some of the time; you can even fool some of the people all the time; but you can't fool all of the people all the time. 99

—**Lincoln**, to a White House visitor, as quoted in *Lincoln's Yarns & Stories* by Colonel Alexander K. McClure, 1901

What is *habeas corpus*, and why did Lincoln suspend it?

Habeas corpus (a Latin phrase literally meaning "you should have the body") is a legal term that refers to a prisoner's right to go before a judge and argue that the manner of his imprisonment was unlawful. The *writ* (that is, written order) of *habeas corpus* is one of the strongest safeguards against violations of a person's civil rights. The writ of *habeas corpus* is guaranteed by the Constitution—except "in cases of rebellion or invasion." In such cases *habeas corpus* may be suspended, or canceled.

From the start of the war, there were many individuals in the North who supported the Confederate cause. Secret societies, such as the Knights of the Golden Circle and the Sons of Liberty, plotted to overthrow the government by cutting telegraph lines, destroying rail lines, and even murdering officials. Though the secret societies did little serious harm to the Union's cause, there was real fear of them in the North. In 1862 Lincoln exercised his power—as he saw it—to suspend *habeas corpus*. Military police could arrest people suspected of treason and hold them without trial indefinitely.

To southerners, Lincoln's action proved what they'd been saying all along—that "Honest Abe" was really a tyrant, a dictator. Even some Republicans were disturbed by the president's order. The Constitution implies that only Congress can suspend *habeas corpus*. However, Congress was not in session at the time, and Lincoln felt he had to act in this time of crisis. His order held, and in 1863 Congress added its formal consent.

Following the attacks of September 11, 2001, the Bush Administration asserted its rights to seize suspected terrorists, deny them access to lawyers, hold them indefinitely, and try them in secret military tribunals rather than in public civil courts. In effect, the Bush Administration suspended the writ of *habeas corpus* for suspected terrorists.

What happened at Gettysburg?

Three times, in 1862 and 1863, the Union tried to take Richmond, Virginia, the capital of the Confederacy. All three times, troops led by General Robert E. Lee turned the Union forces back. The third Union advance ended at the Battle of Chancellorsville, where Lee, commanding about fifty-seven thousand men, defeated a force of about ninety-seven thousand Yankees. The victory at Chancellorsville gave Lee the confidence to launch an invasion of the North.

Gathering reinforcements and marching up the Shenandoah Valley, Lee entered southern Pennsylvania with seventy-five thousand men. Things had never looked worse for the Union.

Near the little town of Gettysburg, Pennsylvania, Lee encountered eighty-three thousand Union soldiers under the command of General George G. Meade. Meade had taken command of the Union troops in the East only days earlier. For three days, July 1–3, 1863, the armies fought savagely. The climactic exchange came when Confederate General George Pickett led a massive charge on Union artillery.

During Pickett's Charge, almost seven thousand Confederates were killed in half an hour. The South's advance had been turned back.

The Battle of Gettysburg left twenty-three thousand dead or wounded Yankees and twenty-eight thousand dead or wounded Rebels. It was the bloodiest battle of the war.

Word of Gettysburg reached Lincoln on the Fourth of July. Three days later, he learned that General Grant had taken Vicksburg, Mississippi, the last major Confederate stronghold on the Mississippi River. At last the war was going the Union's way.

HAPPY THANKSGIVING, PRESIDENT LINCOLN

When Sarah Buell Hale's husband died, leaving her with five children to support, Sarah worked as a writer and magazine editor. She wrote an early abolitionist novel, *Northwood*, and other pieces, but her best-known work is "Mary Had a Little Lamb."

Ever since the late 1700s, Thanksgiving had been celebrated by some American communities at different times and for different reasons. Starting in the 1840s, Sarah Hale used her popular fashion magazine, *Godey's Lady's Book*, to promote Thanksgiving as an official national holiday. She hoped that a day of remembrance and thanks would bridge the ever-widening rift between North and South. For fifteen years Hale lobbied the states and the federal government.

Finally, in October 1863, inspired by Hale and the victory at Gettysburg, Lincoln declared the last Thursday (now the fourth Thursday) in November a permanent national day of Thanksgiving.

Did anyone live at the Gettysburg Address?

Lincoln was not the main speaker at the ceremony dedicating the battlefield cemetery at Gettysburg on November 19, 1863. That honor fell to Edward Everett, a famous orator from Massachusetts. Everett spoke for over two hours; Lincoln for just minutes. But it is Lincoln's spare remarks that have stood the test of time. In a short speech now known as the Gettysburg Address, he summed up what the North was fighting for and why the Union was worth preserving.

AMERICAN VOICES

❝ Four score and seven years ago our fathers brought forth on this continent a new nation, conceived in liberty and dedicated to the proposition that all men are created equal.

"Now we are engaged in a great civil war, testing whether that nation or any nation so conceived and so dedicated can long endure. We are met on a great battlefield of that war. We have come to dedicate a portion of that field as a final resting place for those who here gave their lives that the nation might live. It is altogether fitting and proper that we should do this.

"But in a larger sense, we cannot dedicate, we cannot consecrate, we cannot hallow this ground. The brave men, living and dead who struggled here have consecrated it far above our poor power to add or detract. The world will little note nor long remember what we say here, but it can never forget what they did here. It is for us the living rather to be dedicated here to the unfinished work which they who fought here have thus far so nobly advanced. It is rather for us to be here dedicated to the great task remaining before us—that from these honored dead we take increased devotion to that cause for which they gave the last full measure of devotion—that we here highly resolve that these dead shall not have died in vain, that this nation under God shall have a new birth of freedom, and that government of the people, by the people, for the people shall not perish from the earth. **99**

—**Lincoln**, Gettysburg Address

66 I should be glad, if I could flatter myself that I came as near to the central idea of the occasion, in two hours, as you did in two minutes. **99**

—**Edward Everett**, in a letter to Lincoln written the day after the ceremony at Gettysburg

WHAT IS IT ABOUT ENVELOPES?

Legend tells us that Lincoln wrote out the Gettysburg Address on the back of an envelope.

Did it happen? It's an old story that's still told in some books, but it's not true. Lincoln wrote the speech on official presidential stationery, composing most of it before he arrived in Pennsylvania and finishing it the night before he spoke.

The story of Lincoln and the envelope is similar to the story of how another famous American text was written. While watching the bombardment of Fort McHenry during the War of 1812, Francis Scott Key supposedly composed "The Star-Spangled Banner" on the back of an envelope. All of that story is true—except for the part about the envelope!

Did Lincoln ever find the general he was looking for?

Even after the victory at Gettysburg, Lincoln wasn't happy with the leader of the Army of the Potomac. General Meade did not pursue Lee and his weakened army as they retreated back into Virginia, where they readied to fight again. Upset that the chance to end the war had slipped away, President Lincoln looked to the west to find a new general.

U. S. "Unconditional Surrender" Grant had earned his nickname early in the war because that's what he'd demanded of a Confederate fort. After his victory at Vicksburg, Lincoln increased Grant's command.

Less than four months later, Lincoln, recognizing a military genius, appointed Grant general-in-chief of the Union armies. The man who took Grant's place as commander in the west? General William Tecumseh Sherman.

> ## ULYSSES S. GRANT
>
> Ulysses S. Grant (1822–1885) is sometimes portrayed—in contrast to the saintly image of Robert E. Lee—as a bloodthirsty, cigar-chomping, foul-mouthed, simpleminded drunkard.
>
> In reality Grant was rather bashful, even prudish, and he did not like to see his men die on the battlefield. He may have been an alcoholic—he was known, especially in his youth, to have gone on binges—but he was never drunk at crucial times during the war. As for his intelligence, after serving two largely unsuccessful terms as president he went on to write his *Personal Memoirs*, widely regarded as one of the great works of American literature. It's true, though, that he smoked a lot of cigars; it was throat cancer that killed him.

Was Lincoln a shoo-in for president in 1864?

Today we think of Lincoln as a hero. Some historians consider him the best president in history.

It wasn't always that way. In fact, Lincoln wasn't very popular when he was in office. Back in 1864, with the war dragging on, people had grown tired of all the death and destruction.

Even though the tide of war was slowly turning in the Union's favor, many in the North wanted peace. Some northern Democrats believed that if Lincoln took back the Emancipation Proclamation, the Confederate states might agree to return to the Union. Some radical Republicans, on the other hand, wanted a candidate who would pursue abolitionist ideals even more aggressively than Lincoln did. And though most northerners still opposed slavery in principle, many began to wonder: Why should white men die to liberate blacks?

Despite such opposition, Lincoln managed to retain the Republican candidacy, but the race for president would not be an easy one.

AMERICAN VOICES

" It is best not to swap horses while crossing the river. **"**

—**Lincoln**, on the wisdom of the Republican Party's retaining him as its presidential candidate

How did the Democrats run against Lincoln?

By August Lincoln was convinced he was going to lose the presidency to his former general George B. McClellan, the Democratic candidate. McClellan

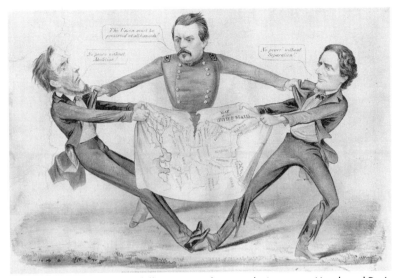

In this pro-McClellan cartoon, the general tries to stop Lincoln and Davis from tearing the nation apart.

promised to respect the "rights of the States" if they would return to the Union. He was in effect offering to undo the Emancipation Proclamation and allow the Confederate states to preserve slavery.

Additionally, the Democratic platform called for an immediate end to the fighting. Even though the Union was winning the war, an armistice, or truce, would have amounted to southern victory.

Some of Lincoln's advisors told him that, if he wanted to win reelection, he would have to drop abolition as a precondition for peace. Let the South have its slaves, they said. Press for peace; win reelection. The Union could still be saved through negotiation.

Lincoln held firm. Even if he *rescinded*, or took back, the Emancipation Proclamation, the South would never return to the Union voluntarily. "We will govern ourselves," Jefferson Davis had declared in July, "if we have to see every Southern plantation sacked, every Southern city in flames."

Lincoln's overriding mission was to save the Union. He knew this could be done only by winning the war. And he believed emancipation was absolutely necessary to the war effort. Over two hundred thousand black soldiers and sailors were enlisted in the Union military. If he broke his promise to free the slaves, he said, "all colored men now in our service would instantly desert us. And rightfully too." He believed the Union war effort couldn't last three weeks without them. Lincoln would keep his promise, even if it meant defeat at the polls.

❝ Still, to use a coarse, but an expressive figure, broken eggs cannot be mended. I have issued the Emancipation Proclamation, and I cannot retract it. **❞**
—**Lincoln**, in a letter from 1863

How did Lincoln win reelection?

As late as the end of August 1864, Lincoln's chances for reelection looked grim. But September 1 changed everything. On that day Sherman captured Atlanta, Georgia.

Now it was clear that Sherman would be able to crush the Deep South. The Union still controlled the entire Mississippi River. Grant was advancing, slowly, on Richmond. For the first time, Union victory seemed absolutely inevitable. Public opinion in the North changed overnight. Why press for peace when victory was so close?

McClellan waffled. He said that peace would come only if the South first agreed to return to the Union.

McClellan went from looking like a man of compromise to looking like a man of little principle. He became the Virginia Creeper all over again. And Lincoln went from zero to hero. In November Lincoln handily won reelection, carrying every state (every northern state, that is—the South didn't participate) except Delaware, Kentucky, and New Jersey. Andrew Johnson would be his vice president.

PRESIDENTIAL VOTE, 1864

Lincoln—2,203,831 (55% of votes)

McClellan—1,797,019 (45% of votes)

What was Sherman's March?

During that same November, General Sherman began his infamous "march to the sea," cutting a swath 60 miles wide and 285 miles long through Georgia. Sherman's sixty-two thousand men destroyed everything in their path from Atlanta to the coastal city of Savannah—rail lines, warehouses, factories, water tanks, barns,

bridges, farm animals, and crops. Everything of any possible use to the enemy was ripped down, torn up, killed, or burned. Sherman's March was intended to cripple and demoralize the South, and it did.

AMERICAN VOICES

❝ War is at best barbarism. . . . Its glory is all moonshine. It is only those who have neither fired a shot nor heard the shrieks and groans of the wounded who cry aloud for blood, more vengeance, more desolation. ❞

—**William Tecumseh Sherman**, in an address at Michigan Military Academy, 1879

What did Lincoln say at his Second Inaugural?

By the time of his Second Inaugural on March 4, 1865, Lincoln was looking ahead to *reconstruction*—putting the nation back together again. The Thirteenth Amendment, abolishing slavery from all of the United States, had already passed through the House and the Senate. It was in the process of being ratified by the states. Abolition was inevitable.

Although the war wasn't over, the end was in sight. Enormous questions faced the nation: Should Confederate veterans be punished? What about Confederate politicians—should they be tried for treason? What should be done for the millions of former slaves, who had no property and little means of supporting themselves?

Lincoln didn't have all the answers yet, but he'd begun groping toward them.

66 Fondly do we hope—fervently do we pray—that this mighty scourge of war may speedily pass away. Yet, if God wills that it continue until all the wealth piled by the bondsman's two hundred and fifty years of unrequited toil shall be sunk, and until every drop of blood drawn by the lash shall be paid by another drawn with the sword, as was said three thousand years ago, so still it must be said, 'The judgments of the Lord are true and righteous altogether.'

"With malice toward none; with charity for all; with firmness in the right, as God gives us to see the right, let us strive on to finish the work we are in; to bind up the nation's wounds; to care for him who shall have borne the battle, and for his widow, and his orphan—to do all which may achieve and cherish a just and lasting peace among ourselves, and with all nations. **99**

—from Lincoln's Second Inaugural Address, March 4, 1865

How did the Civil War end?

As Sherman advanced through Georgia, Confederate General John Bell Hood led one last, desperate offensive up in Tennessee. Hood attempted to cut off Sherman's supply line by taking Nashville. Hood's men were met by Union troops commanded by Major General George H. Thomas. The Battle of Nashville (December 15–16, 1864) resulted in utter defeat for the Rebels.

Lee's exhausted Army of Northern Virginia was the only remaining Confederate force of any size.

On April 1 Grant finally took Petersburg, Virginia. Two days later the Confederates evacuated Richmond. A week after that, on April 9, 1865, Lee surrendered to Grant at the village of Appomattox Court House, Virginia.

Grant was generous in victory. Lee, his officers, and their men would not be held prisoner. They could go home, and they could take their horses and guns with them. Although scattered Confederate forces remained active for several more weeks, the Civil War was essentially over.

CHAPTER 8

Lincoln's Legacy

The Assassination of President Lincoln by Currier & Ives

What happened at Ford's Theatre?

The end of the war brought joy to all of Washington, and especially to the White House. A great task lay ahead of the president: reuniting the nation. In the meantime, the everyday duties of office filled up his hours.

Lincoln spent the day of April 14, 1865, meeting with congressmen and cabinet officers, reviewing documents, receiving visitors, and spending a little time with his family. That evening he and Mary went to see a comedy, *Our American Cousin*, at nearby Ford's Theatre.

The Lincolns arrived late. The performance stopped and the orchestra played "Hail to the Chief" while the Lincolns took their box seats in the balcony.

At about ten P.M. a radical southern sympathizer named John Wilkes Booth snuck up behind Lincoln. Booth raised his pistol and, from point-blank range, fired a bullet into the back of the president's head. Lincoln slumped forward, unconscious. His wife screamed. Booth stabbed a bystander in the arm, then leaped from the balcony to the stage, breaking a bone in his lower leg on impact.

The theater erupted. In the confusion Booth slipped out the stage door, jumped on his waiting horse, and rode away.

Lincoln was carried to a house across the street. He never regained consciousness and died nine hours later, at 7:22 on the morning of April 15, 1865. Within hours Vice President Andrew Johnson was sworn in as the new president.

Presidential Assassinations

Since Lincoln, three other presidents have been assassinated:

James Garfield in 1881, by Charles Guiteau

William McKinley in 1901, by Leon Czolgosz

John F. Kennedy in 1963, by Lee Harvey Oswald

❝ *Sic semper tyrannis!* The South is avenged! **❞**
—**John Wilkes Booth** reportedly shouted this from the stage of Ford's Theatre. *Sic semper tyrannis*, the motto of the state of Virginia since the eighteenth century, is Latin for "Thus always to tyrants."

❝ Now he belongs to the ages. **❞**
—Secretary of War **Edwin Stanton** on the death of Lincoln

❝ I knowed they'd kill him. I ben awaiting fur it. **❞**
—reportedly said by Lincoln's beloved stepmother, **Sarah Johnston Lincoln**, upon hearing news of the assassination

What happened to Booth?

After fleeing Ford's Theatre, Booth rode south out of Washington into the Maryland countryside, where he joined up with a conspirator, David Herold. At four in the morning the pair arrived at the house of Dr. Samuel Mudd, who set Booth's broken leg for him.

For the next week, Booth and Herold hid out in the swamps of southern Maryland, avoiding the federal troops who patrolled the area in search of them. On April 22 they crossed the Potomac River into Virginia, where they expected to be given a hero's welcome. Instead, the local farmers, not wanting to get in trouble, told them to move on.

On April 26—twelve days after the assassination— cavalry soldiers finally found Booth and Herold holed up in a tobacco barn in the Virginia countryside. Herold gave himself up, but Booth refused to come out. He was shot in the neck and killed.

What was the Lincoln Special?

After lying in state in Washington for a week, Lincoln's body was shipped back to Illinois for burial. Decorated with black bunting on the sides and a large photograph of Lincoln over the cowcatcher on the front, the train that carried the body on the meandering sixteen-hundred-mile, two-week journey west was known as the Lincoln Special.

The train passed through hundreds of small towns and was met by millions of mourners. At major stops along the way, Lincoln's coffin was carried to a public space such as a court- or statehouse, where citizens filed past the open coffin to pay their respects. On May 4 Lincoln was laid to rest in Oak Hill Cemetery in Springfield.

The gold, silver, and crystal hearse that carried Lincoln's body in Springfield to Oak Hill Cemetery

What was Lincoln's plan for Reconstruction?

The Civil War had claimed about 620,000 lives. That means about as many Americans died in the Civil War as have been killed in all of America's other wars combined. Most of the war had been fought in Confederate territory. The South was left in ruins.

Lincoln's plan for readmitting former Confederate states to the Union showed his commitment to reconciliation. It called for southerners to take a loyalty oath. When just 10 percent of the voting population of a state had taken the oath, that state was to be readmitted to the Union and could begin to re-form its government. Lincoln didn't favor prosecuting former Confederate officials for treason or other crimes.

How did Reconstruction proceed without Lincoln?

When Lincoln was killed, a split appeared between radical Republicans, who wanted to punish the South more, and northern Democrats, who wanted the softest possible treatment of the South. Ultimately, the issue came down to this: How would freed slaves in the South be treated? Would they have equal civil rights?

Unfortunately, Lincoln's successor, Andrew Johnson, harbored proslavery sentiments. Johnson did everything he could to stop efforts to ensure the civil rights of blacks in the South.

Lincoln would certainly have been more effective at unifying the nation and reconciling people to the new status of black Americans. By the time Johnson was succeeded in 1869 by Ulysses S. Grant, hope for equality between the races was dead. It would be almost a hundred years before blacks would win their full civil rights.

AMERICAN VOICES

O Captain! my Captain! our fearful trip is done,

The ship has weather'd every rack,

the prize we sought is won,

The port is near, the bells I hear,

the people all exulting,

While follow eyes the steady keel,

the vessel grim and daring;

But O heart! heart! heart!

O the bleeding drops of red,

Where on the deck my Captain lies,

Fallen cold and dead.

—Walt Whitman

What became of Mary Lincoln?

The horror of witnessing her husband's violent murder pushed Mary to extremes of grief. For five weeks following the assassination, she didn't leave her darkened room in the White House. Finally, on May 22, 1865, she boarded a train back to Illinois, accompanied by her two sons, Robert and Tad.

Robert was studying law in Chicago, and Mary and Tad lived with him there for several years. Although Mary had inherited money from Abraham, she was terrified, convinced she was on the brink of poverty. She became involved in shady schemes to raise money. The press had never liked her, and even in her widowhood certain newspapers were merciless.

To escape the bad publicity, she and Tad moved to Germany, where Tad attended school for a couple of years. Following a brief stay in England, they returned to Chicago in 1871. Two months later Tad died at the age of eighteen, probably of tuberculosis.

For the rest of her life, Mary alternately hoarded money—once sewing thousands of dollars' worth of bonds into her petticoats—and went on spending sprees. By 1875 Robert, now a prominent lawyer, had become so concerned for—or embarrassed by—her strange behavior that he had her declared legally insane and confined to a hospital.

Mary may have been crazy, but she wasn't stupid. She hired a lawyer (a woman—one of the very few female attorneys of the time) and won her own release after only three months.

For another seven years Mary wandered Europe and America, fearful, increasingly sick, weakened, and nearly blind. On July 16, 1882, at age sixty-three, she died in her sister Elizabeth's home in Springfield, where she'd been married forty years before.

What became of Robert Lincoln?

A married man with three children, Robert had a successful law practice in Chicago. During the 1880s he served as secretary of war under Presidents James Garfield and Chester Arthur. He was later appointed ambassador to England by President Benjamin Harrison. In 1901 Robert

Robert Lincoln, at the Lincoln Memorial dedication ceremony

became president of the Pullman Company, a huge train-car manufacturer. Throughout his career, there was talk of Robert Lincoln as a possible Republican candidate for U.S. president, but he never pursued the post.

In 1922 Robert attended the dedication ceremony of the Lincoln Memorial in Washington, D.C. He died in 1926, at the age of eighty-two. His home, Hildene, in Manchester, Vermont, is now a historic site.

Robert's three children gave him three grandchildren. None of the grandchildren had any children, however, and the last of Abraham Lincoln's direct descendants died in 1985.

BODY SNATCHING

In 1876 gangsters tried to steal Lincoln's corpse from its aboveground tomb in Springfield. The plan was to hold the body ransom and exchange it for the gang leader's release from prison.

The gangsters managed to get Lincoln's coffin halfway out before police, tipped off by an informant, descended on them. The grave robbers ran, but all were captured eventually and served prison time. In 1901 Lincoln's body was buried ten feet underground, safe inside a coffin encased in concrete.

How is Lincoln remembered today?

Thousands of streets, hundreds of schools, and dozens of towns and counties have been named Lincoln. Illinois is known as "The Land of Lincoln," and Kentucky and Indiana claim him as a native son too. His face is on the penny and the five-dollar bill and was sculpted in stone, sixty feet high, on the side of Mount Rushmore.

The Lincoln Memorial in Washington has been a focal point for important Civil Rights events. Marian Anderson, a black opera singer, performed there in

The Lincoln Memorial in Washington, D.C.

1939. The Reverend Dr. Martin Luther King Jr. gave his famous "I Have a Dream" speech on the steps of the Lincoln Memorial in 1963, a hundred years after Lincoln issued the Emancipation Proclamation.

We celebrate Lincoln's and George Washington's birthdays (Washington was born on February 22) jointly on Presidents' Day.

Was Lincoln the greatest president ever?

Lincoln is widely regarded as the finest writer and speechmaker of all the presidents—truly in a class by himself. Many of his offhand quips and witticisms are remembered today.

Some historians have found fault in Lincoln's opinions on race. Others have pointed to his suspension of *habeas corpus*—and to the

Emancipation Proclamation, for that matter—as proof that he had no regard for the Constitution. But most historians consistently rank Lincoln among the top three or four presidents in the nation's history. Many consider him the greatest of all.

Frederick Douglass said of Lincoln, "Born and reared among the lowly, a stranger to wealth and luxury, compelled to grapple single-handed with the flintiest hardships of life, from tender youth to sturdy manhood, he grew strong in the manly and heroic qualities demanded by the great mission to which he was called by the votes of his countrymen."

EQUALITY FOR ALL

The National Association for the Advancement of Colored People (NAACP) was formed on February 12, 1909—the hundredth anniversary of Lincoln's birth.

The famous newspaperman and radical Republican Horace Greeley, friend and sometime opponent of Lincoln, voiced similar sentiments:

"He was not a born king of men . . . but a child of the people, who made himself a great persuader, therefore a leader, by dint of firm resolve, patient effort and dogged perseverance. He slowly won his way to eminence and fame by doing the work that lay next to him—doing it with all his growing might—doing it as well as he could, and learning by his failure, when failure was encountered, how to do it better. . . . He was open to all impressions and influences, and gladly profited by the teachings of events and circumstances, no matter how adverse or unwelcome. There was probably no year of his life when he was not a wiser, cooler and better man than he had been the year preceding."

FEBRUARY 12, 1809	Born in Kentucky
1816	Moves to Indiana
1830	Moves to Illinois
1834	Elected to Illinois House of Representatives
1842	Marries Mary Todd
1846	Elected to U.S. Congress
1856	Joins Republican Party
1858	Loses U.S. Senate race
NOVEMBER 6, 1860	Elected president
DECEMBER 20, 1860	South Carolina secedes; other southern states soon follow
FEBRUARY 9, 1861	Confederate States of America forms, with Jefferson Davis as president
MARCH 4, 1861	Sworn in to office
APRIL 12, 1861	Confederates fire on Fort Sumter, South Carolina; Civil War begins
APRIL 15, 1861	Robert E. Lee declines command of Union forces in the East
JULY 21, 1861	Union army suffers defeat at First Bull Run, Virginia

MARCH 9, 1862	Ironclads *Monitor* and *Merrimac* (renamed *Virginia*) fight to draw at Hampton Roads, Virginia
APRIL 6–7, 1862	Union forces under General Grant score victory at Shiloh, Tennessee
APRIL 24, 1862	Union Admiral David Farragut takes New Orleans, Louisiana
JUNE 1, 1862	Lee assumes command of Confederate forces in the East
JUNE 25–JULY 1, 1862	Union forces under General McClellan are turned back from Richmond at the Seven Days Battle
AUGUST 29–30, 1862	Union forces again suffer defeat, at Second Bull Run
SEPTEMBER 17, 1862	Confederate advance is halted at Antietam, Maryland; single bloodiest day of war leaves twenty-six thousand dead or wounded
SEPTEMBER 22, 1862	Lincoln issues Preliminary Emancipation Proclamation
DECEMBER 13, 1862	Union army is turned away from Richmond following defeat at Fredericksburg
JANUARY 1, 1863	Emancipation Proclamation goes into effect

MAY 4, 1863	Confederate victory at Chancellorsville; for the third time, the Union fails to take Richmond
JULY 1–3, 1863	Battle of Gettysburg marks South's deepest penetration into Union territory
JULY 4, 1863	Grant captures Vicksburg, Mississippi
SEPTEMBER 19–20, 1863	Confederates score victory at Chickamauga, Georgia; defeated Union forces become surrounded at nearby Chattanooga, Tennessee
OCTOBER 16, 1863	Grant assumes command of entire western theater
NOVEMBER 19, 1863	Gettysburg Address
NOVEMBER 23–25, 1863	Troops under Grant defeat the Confederates at Chattanooga, liberating the Union soldiers trapped there
MARCH 9, 1864	Lincoln appoints Grant head of entire Union army
MAY 4, 1864	Beginning of final Union advance into South; Grant leads forces in Virginia, while General Sherman leads forces in Tennessee

JUNE 15, 1864	Nine-month Union siege of Petersburg, Virginia, begins
SEPTEMBER 2, 1864	Sherman takes Atlanta, Georgia
NOVEMBER 8, 1864	Lincoln wins reelection
NOVEMBER 15, 1864	Sherman begins his march to the sea through Georgia
JANUARY 31, 1865	Congress approves Thirteenth Amendment, abolishing slavery, to the Constitution; amendment must be ratified by states before it becomes law
APRIL 2, 1865	Grant takes Petersburg
APRIL 3, 1865	Grant enters Richmond
APRIL 9, 1865	Lee surrenders, effectively ending the Civil War
APRIL 14, 1865	Lincoln assassinated at Ford's Theatre in Washington, D.C., by John Wilkes Booth
APRIL 15, 1865	Lincoln dies
MAY 1865	Remaining scattered Confederate forces surrender
DECEMBER 16, 1865	Thirteenth Amendment ratified; slavery abolished

NONFICTION

Following are several nonfiction books for young readers that center on different aspects of Lincoln's life and times.

Freedman, Russell A. *Lincoln: A Photobiography*. Boston: Houghton Mifflin, 1987.

Holzer, Harold. *Abraham Lincoln the Writer: A Treasury of His Greatest Speeches and Letters*. Honesdale, Pa.: Boyds Mill Press, 2000.

Sandburg, Carl. *Abraham Lincoln: The Prairie Years & the War Years: The Definitive One-Volume Biography*. New York: Galahad Books, 1999. For older readers, a one-volume condensation of Sandburg's famous six-volume biography, first published in the 1920s and 1930s.

Somerlott, Robert. *The Lincoln Assassination in American History*. Berkeley Heights, N.J.: Enslow, 1998.

FICTION

Following are novels for young readers set during the Civil War.

Denenberg, Barry. *When Will This Cruel War Be Over? The Civil War Diary of Emma Simpson, Gordonsville, Virginia, 1864*. New York: Scholastic, 1996.

Hesse, Karen. *A Light in the Storm: The Civil War Diary of Amelia Martin, Fenwick Island, Delaware, 1861*. New York: Scholastic, 1999.

Hunt, Irene. *Across Five Aprils*. New York: Follet, 1964.

Keith, Harold. *Rifles for Watie*. New York: Crowell, 1957.

Lyons, Mary E., and Muriel M. Branch. *Dear Ellen Bee: A Civil War Scrapbook of Two Union Spies*. New York: Atheneum, 2000.

Reit, Seymour. *Behind Rebel Lines: The Incredible Story of Emma Edmonds, Civil War Spy*. Madison, Wis.: Turtleback Books, 2001.

Colbert, David, ed. *Eyewitness to America: 500 Years of America in the Words of Those Who Saw It Happen.* New York: Pantheon Books, 1997.

Davis, Kenneth C. *Don't Know Much About® the Civil War.* New York: Morrow, 1996.

——. *Don't Know Much About® History.* New York: Crown, 1990.

Donald, David Herbert. *Lincoln.* New York: Simon & Schuster, 1995.

Franklin, John Hope, and Alfred A. Moss, Jr. *From Slavery to Freedom: A History of Negro Americans.* 6th ed. New York: Knopf, 1988.

Heffner, Richard D., ed. *A Documentary History of the United States.* 4th ed. New York: New American Library, 1985.

Lang, J. Stephen. *Drawn to the Civil War.* Winston-Salem, N.C.: John F. Blair, 1999.

McPherson, James M. *Battle Cry of Freedom: The Civil War Era.* New York: Oxford University Press, 1988.

Miller, William Lee. *Lincoln's Virtues: An Ethical Biography.* New York: Knopf, 2002.

Ricks, Christopher, and William L. Vance, eds. *The Faber Book of America.* London and Boston: Faber and Faber, 1992.

Thomas, Benjamin P. *Abraham Lincoln: A Biography.* New York: Knopf, 1952.

Wills, Garry. *Lincoln at Gettysburg: The Words That Remade America.* New York: Simon & Schuster, 1992.

NOTE: References to illustrations are in *italics*.